Through My Trifocals Backward

Irma "Grams" Fisher

Through My Trifocals Backward, by Irma "Grams" Fisher. ISBN 978-1-62137-650-7 (Softcover) 978-1-62137-651-4 (eBook)

Library of Congress Control Number: 2015900482

Artwork by Bill and Susan Mrosek

To my family
who stimulate and encourage me
and urge me on
with many, many thanks.

And credit to Anna Mirocha,
who did a wonderful job editing
these memoirs.

Contents

PART ONE

ME AND MY EARLY S.O.'s (SIGNIFICANT OTHERS)

BEFORE THE BEGINNING

I remember the very time I was born. People don't believe me, but it's true. It was October 7, 1921, between the two World Wars when Harding was president. I couldn't help but remember because my parents talked about my birth all the time when I was still in the womb—which, yes, I couldn't help but remember—like, "The doctor said in a couple of months," then, "The doctor said a couple of weeks," and then, it was down to days. Then it finally happened like this:

The cocoon I lived in had a lot of space when I was first there, but then it seemed to shrink and become very crowded. I tried to make it wider by hitting the walls with my elbows, hands and feet, but that didn't really help. Nonetheless, on the day I was born I was floating around as much as I could in my little space, and I was having a great old relaxing time when suddenly there was an earthquake. It was ghastly. Tossed me up, dropped me down, but mostly crushed me and squashed me until I thought I'd never get back into my shape again. It lasted and lasted, almost forever, and I was exhausted and angry.

Who was doing this and why? I liked my dark, quiet, floaty place.

Then things began to ease off, but only for a moment. All at once I felt a rush, a gush, and I was suddenly thrust out into nothingness. I closed my eyes tight as tight could be and vowed not to open them as long as that terrible, hurtful bright light kept shining all around me. I noticed at once that my little cocoon-like home was gone. I kept flinging my arms and legs about, trying to find something I could grab hold of, but there was nothing. Instead, somebody grabbed me—by my legs—and swatted my bottom while swinging me in the breeze in a rude, indecent way. I wanted to wriggle back to where I came from, but I couldn't.

Suddenly, without warning, someone clamped my finger, stuck things up my nose and in my throat. I was attacked all over. I was flung upside down and sideways, I was terrified and didn't know what to do. There were loud noises, very loud, not the mellow muffled, hushed sounds of my floaty home. Is that what I had to do to make this painful, vibrating noise stop—make noises of my own? I tried some grunts and squeaks with no success. It had to be louder. I tried a little cry. They thought it was cute. "How about a lusty yowl?" I thought. I made it very lusty, and that did it! Some warm wet stuff was smoothed all over me and it felt good. Something soft and warm was wrapped tightly around me and soon I was floating back and forth, back and forth, almost like before. Everything was hushed. The light was dimmed. Something was stuck in my mouth, which made me scared at first, but then I sucked on it and it tasted pretty good. I got sleepy, relaxed and happy. I thought, "If I have to leave that other place, this one may not be so bad. I'll give it a shot."

And I did. That's what I know happened and how I got here, and so far it's been good.

CHAPTER 1

AT THE START

Everyone agreed I came into the world on October 7, 1921, in Buffalo, New York, feet first, and that they've been solidly on the ground ever since. No, it wasn't a natural breech birth; it was Dr. Potter. He was written up in medical journals for turning all the babies he delivered so they emerged

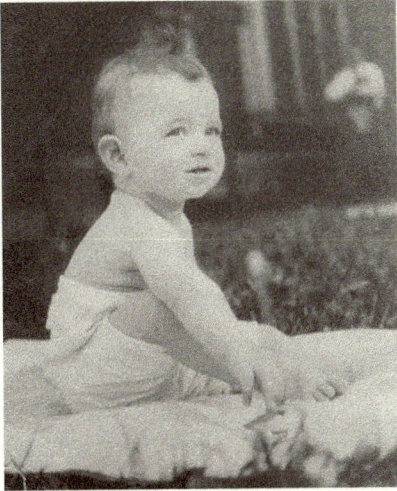

Infant Irma

feet first. It made their heads stay nice and round. My mother never told me how she felt about this procedure, and I never thought to ask. There was no point asking my father, because he wasn't even in Dr. Potter's house with mother during my birth. He was off

Irma at nine months.

making arrangements to bury my great uncle, who died

1

the day I was born. Dad handled difficult problems, like surgeries and terminal illnesses, for everyone—family and friends alike. Though he was a lawyer, not a doctor, he was always the responsible one. So, like the saying in the old story, "The shoemaker's children had no shoes," Dad wasn't there on my big day—and my mother's (it was a big day for her because I was their first child). I arrived two years before my brother, Bob, who entered the world the same way, feet first.

Due to badly infected ears, and before antibiotics, I had to have double mastoid surgery at the tender age of two. I had finally grown enough hair to be recognized as a girl, and then they went and shaved it off. Of course, I have no memory of the whole thing, but the arguments I heard later had to do with whether the doctor was too drunk when he operated, or not drunk enough. They agreed I'd kicked him in the stomach, but that was after the surgery, so I couldn't blame my hearing problem on him. Whatever—I ended up with virtually no hearing in one ear, and low normal hearing in the other. That's not as big a problem as it sounds, because I have very good listening—better than most—so I don't think I miss more than anyone else.

By the time I was four, I was gorgeous. I had to be, because I was the flower girl at my Uncle Sam's wedding.

I wore make-up for the first time and fell in love with Maury, the ring bearer, who was five or six. I don't remember Uncle Sam being there, but the bride, Aunt Jean, was a knockout. She was the beauty I wanted to be when I got married—blonde hair, blue eyes, pretty as a picture, and with a figure that filled her spectacular wedding gown like a model's. (I could bleach my brown hair blond, I thought, but I couldn't change my brown eyes.) The train on Aunt Jean's gown took at least a half-hour to catch up with her after she turned the bend when she left temple. I watched every second of it, starry eyed.

When I was in third grade, a renowned specialist decided I had tuberculosis. I was only allowed to go to school half-days because of my low-grade fever every afternoon and evening. I was confined to bed when I wasn't in school, which was dreadfully boring. I did an awful lot of reading, even card-cataloged the books. Then my mother, brother and I moved to sunny Arizona for nine months because it had the climate to cure TB, consumption, allergies and asthma. It was beastly hot there. No air-conditioning yet, or even swamp cooling. We put wet sheets on the windows and had fans blow through them.

After a year of no change in my health, and the persistence of our social-worker cousin in Baltimore, Mother agreed to take me to John's Hopkins, where they discovered the infected remainder of a tonsil. After my second tonsillectomy, they got it all out, the fever was gone and my "TB" miraculously disappeared.

Then it was curvature of the spine, which meant I wasn't allowed to go horseback riding, row a boat or dive—all of which kept me from being in the swing with other kids at camp. It's a wonder my parents and the doctors didn't turn me into an invalid; it sure wasn't for lack of trying. I was a high-risk, costly kid! Who would have thought I'd still be hanging around in my ninth decade!

Irma and Bob

Mother tried to help me overcome my difficult beginnings. I thought she was punishing me. She forced me to take all kinds of lessons: singing, dancing, dramatics, piano and elocution. I didn't want any of them. It was torture!

"Mother, make her stop!" Bobby screamed, with his hands over his ears, as he was being tormented by my vocal renditions during singing lessons. Unfortunately for him, he had a good ear for music and I had a bad voice for it. My singing teacher was a short, fat man, formerly in opera. I had to sing love songs with him when he should have been crooning to his beautiful wife, Carmen. My warbling was painful to the listener *and* no picnic for me. Finally, we went to the Eastman School of Music in Rochester, New York, where I had to sing in front of a dour man whose handlebar mustache and face fell almost to the floor. Mother wanted to know if I had talent. Bobby and I knew the answer, and the sour man agreed with us. He spoke the beautiful two words: "no talent." Saved! I could stop singing. That was one of the happiest days of my life . . . and Bobby's, too.

Mother wasn't aspiring to make me an opera singer, she said, but to help me avoid speaking in a total monotone because of my hearing loss. Makes sense to me now, but I didn't believe it then. I finally escaped from elocution, dancing and dramatics classes, then piano. I thought these trials and tribulations would never end, but they did . . . scarcely a gasp before I reached adulthood.

CHAPTER 2

BROTHER BOB: PART I

The Early Years

"Mother!" I screeched, "Get him out of here!"
There he was, my brother Bob, standing in the living

room telling my date
what I had written in
my diary about him! I
don't know where or
when he got my diary,
but it was off limits,
personal and private,
and this was decidedly
grounds for corporal
punishment. I wanted
to throttle him and

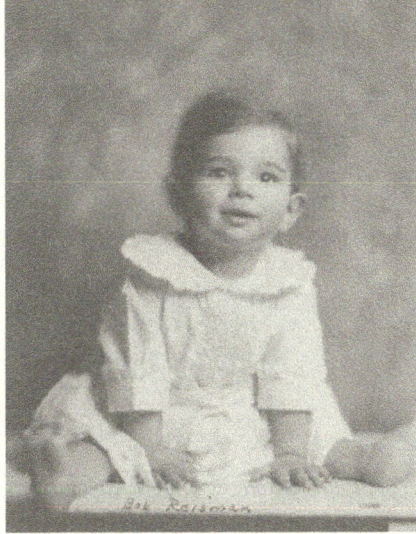

Infant Bobby

would have, but I didn't want to cover my date in blood. I
was always on time for my dates thereafter, not out of
consideration for them but as protection for me. This was
Bob's kid-brother mode. I guess he had a right to act like
the *kid* brother since he was born two years after me on
January 8, 1924.

One of my earliest memories of Bobby is seeing him as a baby in his bathing suit on the sand at Crystal Beach, Canada, responding to anyone walking by asking, "How big is my baby?" He stretched his little arms over his head as high as he could reach and said proudly in a loud voice, "So big!" He was adorable. Everybody liked him and he liked everybody. He was sweet, had a good sense of humor and was fun to be with.

In his role as lovable brother, he helped me talk Mother into letting me stop some of the classes she'd been forcing me to take. We also had fun jitterbugging together. As he threw me out of his arms with a vengeance (always managing to retrieve me), he kept saying, "Now, Irma, you only get out of it what you put into it." He came to a dance at my college, Western Reserve University, and invited me to his dance at Allegheny State College where he was majoring in philosophy. I was proud to have him as my escort and showed him off to all my friends. Best of all, when we were younger, he drank my milk surreptitiously so that mother wouldn't notice because I hated it and he loved it and we never got caught. And when we had to go to bed before we were tired, we tapped melodic rhythms on the common wall between our bedrooms so we could guess which songs they were. That was my sweet, wonderful brother Bob.

Bob had a stubborn streak that frequently came out at the dinner table. It was mandatory, as we were growing up, for the family to be together at dinnertime and to participate in discussions at the table. Any statements made with authority were to be supported, if challenged, by a source that could be quoted. Dinner was not to be interrupted by phone calls or other distractions, but we could leave our seats briefly to collect our sources: the dictionary, encyclopedia, etc. A very early example of Bob's stubbornness came out in a heated discussion about the spelling of the month of February. Bobby, the future English lit professor, was insistent that it had only one "r," that being the last one. Even when confronted with the dictionary and calendar, he refused to change his mind. His spelling was pretty awful all his life, but his writing and pontificating were awesome. Too bad he wasn't into computers. They would do his spelling for him.

Bob hated fighting, even refused to defend himself in case he might hurt the other guy. When he was in elementary school, he wouldn't protect himself against the bully next door, Roger, who plagued him mercilessly. Bob was bigger than Roger, although they were the same age. I had to walk my kid brother to grade school to protect him until Roger picked a fight with Bob, as usual. Bob dodged and sparred with the air but didn't fight, as usual. Roger had his tongue out when he was concentrating, as usual. Bob rose from his crouched position, hitting Roger's chin with his head. Blood spurted from the two teeth flaps in Roger's tongue, and Bobby, not Roger, cried. Then they became fast friends. Roger never bullied Bob again. Ironically, Bob ended up fighting and being injured in two wars: World War II and the siege on Jerusalem during Israel's War for Independence.

School tests were also stressful for Bob, particularly the New York State High School regent's exams. They were daunting even to thick-skinned students. The strain of worry caused Bob stomach upsets and migraines. The test was so intimidating that I caught him writing the Spanish vocabulary in the palm of his hand the day he was to take it. I was horrified. If you were found cheating on an exam, even the very last one in your senior year, all the previous four years of testing were disqualified as though they had never been. I told this to Bobby and pleaded with him to scrub the evidence off before leaving for school. He refused. He was adamant; I was a nervous wreck. He wasn't caught. I don't know if it was because he took my advice or he was just lucky but it was a relief.

Bennett High School, our school, had a large student body. It was like an impersonal factory. There was no individual attention available to students who wanted or needed it. Nonetheless, Dad and I felt it was a good training ground for the real world. Mother disagreed and wanted Bob transferred to a private school, Nichols High School. Mother won the tug of war, and it was good that she did. Bob's grades, which were mediocre at Bennett, soared at his new school, as did his interest in academics and studying. He always liked to learn, and now he could ... and I don't remember him participating in team sports until he switched high schools. I *do* remember him being a champion backstroke swimmer at Boy Scout camp. Then when he transferred to Nichols, he was relaxed enough to play field hockey.

Competitive in sports or games, Bobby always wanted to be the winner. Not unusual … most people like to be winners. Yet he could handle losing, except when he was playing against Dad. I can still picture their hot Ping-Pong games. Dad stood in one spot, moving his paddle from side to side, up and down. Bob, in beautiful and impressive form, ran all around the table, arms swinging, making spectacular shots but rarely enough to win. The little kid in him continued to want to beat Dad even when he grew to adulthood. It was bowling at that time. Dad's form was awful—off balance, as though he was going to skid or slide down the alley after the ball. Bobby's form was beautiful, graceful, flowing, everything right—and Dad won most of the time. It was hard to beat his 260-plus games.

Bob in high school.

Bob was fond of all cultural activities, much to Mother's delight (she had given up on me in that arena). He spouted

Shakespeare, played Caruso records ad nauseam, had a good ear for music, enjoyed the classics and had a fine appreciation of art. He was a prolific, critical reader and had an awareness and vital interest in what was happening around the world.

Although he was two years my junior, and our friends were always different, we had great times together. He taught me all of his summer-camp songs, which I have diligently passed on to my children, grandchildren, and great grandchildren.

Bob's college education was interrupted during

GI Bob

World War II, when he and some of his friends enlisted in the army radio corps before being conscripted. He later volunteered in the glider patrol, then became a paratrooper because the glider patrol was looked upon as "the widow maker." He was in the European Theater and sang the praises of General Patton, to whom he owed his life. Patton, always at the front in battle, continuously overran Bob's outfit's position, making it safer for Bob.

His worst experience was when he and three other men from his outfit were the first to enter Dachau, one of the concentration camps. It took many years before he would talk about seeing the mounds of skeletal bodies, some of them moving, and the stench. It still profoundly pained him that he and his colleagues had inadvertently killed a few people by giving them something to eat, not realizing that the starving victims could not tolerate it. He had nightmares for the rest of his life about that experience. He was discharged after being injured in hand-to-hand combat with a German soldier. And this was the boy who hated to fight.

CHAPTER 3

MY PARENTS

One rainy day when I was in my teens, my brother Bob and I were browsing in the attic and came upon a real treasure. It was a diary in our father's hand, written when he was sixteen. Without compunction, we read it. The most fascinating entry began, "I have just met the girl I am going to marry," whereupon he described our mother. He wrote she was vivacious, vibrant, beautiful, appealing. It took him nine years to make his marriage prediction come true.

Mom and Dad courting.

Over time I learned about their courting days, chiefly from Aunt Mabel, Mother's older sister. She claimed credit for selecting Dad as Mother's mate. Mother had many beaus, but only one main contender with whom my father had to compete. Joe was established and financially secure, and he lavished mother with flowers and candy every time he came to call. Dad's family was poor. He had to work while he was attending law school, and whatever he earned that he didn't need to live on went to his family. It was my aunt's job to chaperone the couples, and she took it seriously. When Joe came courting, my Aunt ate his candy and never left them alone for even a minute. When Dad came to call, she saw to it he had some of Joe's candy and she found reasons to be out of the room during his visits, at least for short periods of time. She liked Dad and was determined to have him, not Joe, as her brother-in-law. This wouldn't have worked if Mother hadn't colluded with her.

Mother and Dad were born an hour apart on June 9, 1895, and they married on their birthday. Nobody ever described their wedding, and I wasn't smart enough to ask about it when there were folks around who had the answers. I do know they had a wonderful marriage, and mother was the envy of all her friends because Dad doted on her.

Dad was a romantic. He kept dance cards dating as far back as high school, each reflecting several dances with my aunt, some with Mother's cousins, the majority

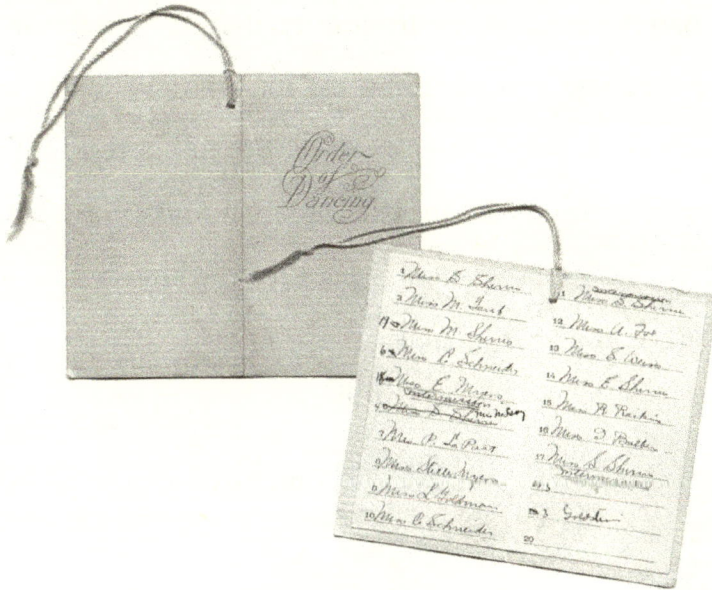

Dad's dance card.

with Mother. Great strategy, smart man! His old ledgers recorded money transactions that took place before—and a number of years after—he was married. They included small loans and repayments made by Mother, some of her relatives, and some of his. He even itemized payments he made to completely furnish both his first law office and his first home, before moving in to either place. These were sizable expenditures for a young lawyer just going into practice and the purchases were completely financed by the bank. When Dad told the people at the bank what he wanted and why, they asked what he had as collateral. He had nothing, but he responded that his future was unlimited and they gave him the full amount! Those were the good old days! An entry of particular interest to me showed what he paid the doctor when I was born. It was not much more than what I paid for the lotions I used when I had my own children.

Dad on the farm.

Dad was a dapper, meticulous man who, as a gentleman farmer, was chided that he was the only person in captivity who could till the soil, dig potatoes and still have the original crease in the trousers of his coveralls or jeans. He spent a large percentage of his time picking up after mother. She hung her clothes on the floor and broadcast all ingredients and utensils over the entire kitchen when she prepared her very tasty dishes. He waited on her, spoiled her rotten, until her death in December 1953. Her zest for life and her decision to live it to the fullest masked how ill she really was. But not from Dad; he knew. The doctors

Mother on the farm.

stated over many, many years that she was "living on a keg of dynamite" and could die at any moment. This was incredible to those who knew her and still couldn't keep up with her, including me. She refused to be made an invalid. Her death at a young fifty-eight was much too soon, but she packed more into her years than most people who lived two or three decades longer. People of all ages and walks of life gravitated to her like bees to honey. She was always as Dad had originally described her—vivacious and vibrant—and she was always his sweetheart.

CHAPTER 4

MY COOKIE-JAR GRANDMA

No room fresheners or incense needed here. Nothing could equal the titillating aroma, the mouthwatering fragrance of a savory blend of such delectables as bagels, brownies, strudel, and more, wafting up from a certain basement apartment. A sweet, round, diminutive lady, with a gray braid circling her head like a

Grandma Sherris

crown, was the gourmet cook responsible for the appetizing scent. My maternal grandma was my "cookie-jar grandma." Her week revolved around her cooking. As far back as my beginning memories, she prepared treats weekly for her four children, gradually adding her eight grandchildren. Twelve huge bags of delicious food were ready for "take-out" every Friday. The staples were the baked goods already mentioned, along with cupcakes, gefilte fish, and one special dish for a dinner, such as sweet and sour stuffed cabbage, or tzimmis, or cheese or meat blintzes. My favorite was tzibili kuchen, a bagel-type dough shaped like a pizza with softened onions covering the entire top. It was to die for, and—sadly—it has never been replicated. None of her dishes could be reproduced, because a "bissel" is not an exact measurement, the kitchen was off limits to one and all, and there was no such thing as a recipe.

All of these creations were made in her one-person, miniscule kitchen, with no help until her children insisted she have a companion. That was when she was 89, two years before she died. Even then, her companion was not allowed in the kitchen but was only permitted to package the goodies after they were produced. Her week, her life, revolved around fashioning these gifts of love.

There were certain days for grocery shopping, others for picking up the boxes that Woolworth's conscientiously saved for her, and then the hours spent cooking. She didn't drive a car, so at the start, she walked and carried her purchases home in her arms. As the family grew, so did the number of items to carry, so she used a cart. When it was still too much to carry she had the stores deliver, but that wasn't satisfactory because she wanted to select the items herself. At that point, my mother chauffeured her.

When my mother predeceased her by six months, I became the chauffeur. That's how I became privy to her schedule, and how I witnessed Grandma's suspenseful procurement of fish. They were kept on ice in fairly high barrels at the market. She considered the fish in front of the store suspect, though I never knew why, so she foraged about in the barrels in a room in the back. The choice fish were those near the bottom. My short little grandma was at risk of plunging headlong into the icy, malodorous depths below. I always feared that one day all I would see of her were her small feet kicking out of the top of the barrel. Fortunately, that never came to pass.

Grandma's mail-order system was comprehensive. All of the wares that could survive the postal system reached the army bases or dormitories, so grandchildren missed nothing by being out of town. The girls at my dorm were familiar with Grandma's goodies and, when the box came in, it was announced on the PA system, "Irma, your grandma is here." If I wasn't fast enough, I would end up with crumbs. No respect!

The great-grandchildren, who were fortunate enough to know and remember Grandma, have the same

JoAnn and Scott at Grandma's.

fond memories their parents do of the candy containers, always full of sweet delights, and the small copper saucers or ashtrays that were marvelous to teeth on and use as cymbals. They kept us occupied while we visited on "pick-up" days.

Grandma migrated to the States from Lithuania when she was in her twenties. For reasons not known to us, her parents did not approve the man she loved, so—as pre-arranged by them—she reluctantly and dutifully married Grandpa, her cousin. He preceded her to this country. They were married in New York state. From then on, Grandma refused any contact with her mother.

Grandma and Grandpa Sherris

We were amazed that this most loving, accepting, nonjudgmental person could cut herself off in this way. She was a good wife to a very talented, bright but difficult man. Grandpa had a hot temper and was insanely jealous when it came to Grandma, even of her affections and time devoted to her children and grandchildren. For that reason, our pick-up times always took place while Grandpa was busy in his tailor shop. He died a short time after their fiftieth wedding anniversary. Although she had never complained about him, the years that followed his death seemed more relaxed for Grandma. I know they were for many of the other family members. The aura of love and acceptance that emanated from Grandma radiated back to her from everyone she met.

Her cooking and keeping up with the "soaps" left little time to visit. I don't know when she found time to crochet the doilies and, most particularly, the banquet-size tablecloths, she made for each grandchild. My crocheted cloth graces my table on all State occasions. Yet I see her in my mind's eye on the rare occasions when she did visit in my home. She is sitting on the edge of the chair with her white-gloved hands folded over the purse

Grandma Sherris in her flowered hat.

in her lap. The hat on her lovely white hair is crowned with cloth flowers. Her face, with the unwrinkled, unblemished complexion of a young girl, glows with *nachas* (the pleasure and pride that parents feel for their children) as she *kvells* (smiles with uncontainable delight). And her children and grandchildren kvell over Grandma. What a privilege she was!

CHAPTER 5

MY EDUCATED GRANDMA

She'd just returned from class. She wanted to be a real American, and to that end she was learning English. She was proud of what she was doing and liked to show off. Her son and his friends, who'd just walked in, became her audience. She decided she'd impress them.

"Hi, Ma," called her son.

"Hello, boys," she responded.

"What's new, Ma? What did you do today?"

"Oy vay, I got *tsuris* [problems]."

"What happened?"

"I couldn't *vawsh* the *vesh*."

"Why couldn't you wash the clothes?" Barney, her son, translated for the benefit of his non-Jewish friend.

"The machine broke down."

"Why didn't you call someone to come and fix it?"

"I did. I called that nice *maven* [expert, skilled in everything]. He came right over to menstruate a new washing machine."

"Good!" the boys sputtered as they beat a hasty retreat. They didn't *explode* until they were out of her hearing.

Grandma Reisman

That was my paternal grandmother, and one of the many stories told about her by my eye- and ear-witness father. He told me how she got a black eye breaking up a fight between him and his older brother. The grandma that I knew could take on a regiment, I figured. She was an Amazonish-looking woman, or put more kindly, she was the picture of an ample peasant woman from the old country. She also would have made a great top sergeant in any man's army. I

Grandpa Reisman

never heard her call Grandpa by his first name, or even *talk* to him. I only remember her *commanding* him by his last name. Anyway, that's how she looked to me. The delicate and beautiful lace tatting that she did with speed and accuracy simply didn't compute with my image of her. And, in my mind, she certainly hadn't had a life before I knew her.

Grandma Reisman at 18.

How wrong I was! Once I began to research our genealogy, I was appalled to learn that Grandma was only seventeen when she came to this country to marry Grandpa—who was an old man of thirty-one. She came from what was Germany, Poland, or Russia according to the time of day and the day of the week. I don't know how she connected with Grandpa. He came from Bessarabia. It probably was an arranged marriage. Maybe she was a mail-order bride. I don't know whether she came alone or with Grandpa. There were no plane flights in those days, just a very long,

Young Grandpa Reisman

tedious boat trip to a new land where she didn't know the language or customs (or perhaps not even Grandpa). Why didn't I think to ask questions about these things, and many more, when I had the chance? Too late now.

Grandpa was a handsome, kind, gentle, soft-spoken man. Actually, I am only guessing that he was soft-spoken. I don't ever remember hearing the sound of his voice. I do remember sitting on his lap, which was relaxing and comforting. I also remember the smell of his cigars, which he smoked perpetually. I still like their scent.

Grandma had twin boys when she was eighteen. One was stillborn and the other died of pneumonia before a year was out. By the time she was in her late twenties, she had five more children. One died later of rheumatic fever at age sixteen.

Seders were held at Grandma's house. No one ever said "Grandpa's house," though I don't know why. Those occasions were

Reisman seder, 1927

my first memories of *her* house, and they were a mixed bag. The food and fun with my cousins was good. The dark wood, dark furniture, old dark darkness was sobering and scary. My other early memory of that house was when Grandpa died. I was eight and it was my first experience with death; it was done in the orthodox Jewish fashion with the mirrors covered, pictures turned to the wall, ghostly, eerie, frightening.

But being with grandma was not all sobering. Dad's family had a quirky sense of humor—laughed at appropriate times, frequently at inappropriate times, like funerals, and often at themselves. I was visiting with Grandma one typical Buffalo winter day and commented on how icy it was outside. She chuckled, then went into a full-blown belly laugh.

"What's so funny, Grandma? What's the big joke?"

After a few minutes she regained her composure sufficiently to talk.

"*A'moliga tzeiten* [once a long time ago], Grandpa and I were walking home on ice from the grocery store. We were shlepping big, heavy grocery bags. In *mitten derinnen* [in the middle of everything], I slipped and fell, such a klutz. The food spilled everywhere. What a mish mash! I laughed. I couldn't stand because I couldn't stop laughing. Grandpa put down his bags so he could help me. A *nechtiger tog*! [Who are you kidding?!] He reached over to take my arm, started to slip, laughed, and landed next to me." She was off again laughing uproariously at the memory. Finally, she continued.

"We sat in the ice and snow like a couple of *mushugges* [crazy people] with groceries all over. *Gottenyu*! [Oh dear God!] You never saw such a mess. We tried to get up, slipped and fell back down. We laughed so hard we almost *plotst* [burst]! The snow was a *metsieh* [lucky break]. We had to crawl to get on it in order to stand. When we finally got everything home, we were *oysgematert* [exhausted]."

Picturing my relatively diminutive grandpa trying to help my hefty grandma to her feet simply cracked me up. What a picture it was to behold!

A part of their humor was inadvertent. It was fallout from their notorious lack of tact. They often talked about people right in front of them, as though they were invisible or deaf. I don't think any of the victims of their lack of diplomacy were amused, but most of the family took it good-naturedly. Mother was the exception. She did not appreciate Dad's comment, "Talking to you is like talking to nobody" when he was complimenting her on being able to maintain a confidence. He realized how that sounded only after he saw her irritation. She would have accepted his apology for ineptness more quickly if he hadn't been laughing.

In the last years of her life, Grandma went from doctor to doctor with complaints, only to be told it was in her head. They thought she was a hypochondriac. She wasn't. She was riddled with cancer, from which she died at the age of seventy-two. The last time I saw her, she was delirious with pain, and she was yelling: "Doctor, doctor, the baby is coming!" If she had to suffer pain, that was at least a good outlook because, if it had been a baby, there was a happy light at the end of the tunnel. Hopefully, that's the way it was for her.

CHAPTER 6

FIRST DEATH

Bobby and I were reminiscing while Donny, my thirteen-year-old nephew, was watching TV in the other room.

I said, "Do you remember, Bob, when I was eight and you were six and it was a Sunday, the day we always climbed into Mom and Dad's bed and sang and talked about what happened all week? The Sunday we dashed to the door, knocked, and ran in without waiting for an answer, and Dad wasn't there?"

"Where's Dad?" we asked.

"At Grandma's," Mom whispered.

"How come?" we asked.

"Grandpa died," she whispered.

"How come?" we whispered.

"He was old and very sick," she whispered.

"Why did Daddy have to go to Grandma's?" we whispered.

"He is helping Grandma make arrangements for the funeral," she whispered.

"Are we going to Grandma's?" we whispered.

"Why are you whispering?" Mom whispered.

"Because grandpa died," we whispered.

When Mom finally stopped laughing she said, "I'm not whispering because Grandpa died. I have laryngitis."

When I was done with this story, Bob collapsed with laughter because he hadn't remembered. His laughter was so contagious I joined him. That's when Donny came in asking what was so funny and Bob gasped.

"We were talking about when our grandfather died."

He asked, "What kind of crazy family do I have? They laugh over what sane people consider sadness. What's wrong with my father and aunt?"

I guess Donny had a right to be disgusted. He was right—and he was wrong. Oh well, he'll learn. He may laugh over my death someday. It won't bother me anymore than it did Grandpa.

CHAPTER 7

MAIDS AND STATUS

Maids brought me up! It wasn't that I had no mother and father, because I certainly did, but it was *because* I had a mother and father that I was brought up by maids. Mother pretended to be sick. She played it to the hilt. I was convinced it was simply a charade that allowed her to indulge herself. Dad encouraged it; he spoiled her rotten. Not only was her every wish his command, but he anticipated her wishes and fulfilled them before she had time to think them up.

Mother, 1936

The things she did were those she enjoyed and wanted to do. She cooked and did it well. Never cleaned or picked up after herself. Didn't have to. Never made a bed, mopped a floor, scoured a sink, or did any of the usual domestic tasks. The maids—and Bob, Dad, and I—were the mop-up team. She loved to shop—clothes, jewelry, tsatskies—whatever struck her fancy at the moment. She delighted in changing the furniture around, usually right after I got used to the last transformation. Let me be accurate. *She* didn't move the furniture, she simply ordered and supervised the operation. She spent the morning on the phone planning the activities of the day, which would include a movie, stage play, symphony, class or lecture, and, on the weekends, dances or parties. Once she got out of bed, it was go, go, go until at least midnight.

Mom and dad, 1914

And so we had maids who did the domestic chores, gave us breakfast, packed our lunches, and were there to listen to the trials and tribulations or the enthusiastic recounting of our days at school. We told them our innermost secrets and they passed along their wisdom to us. I was much more closely aligned with them than with Mother, which resulted in her admonishing me not to "spoil the help." I found it increasingly uncomfortable to have "the help" do things for us that we could surely do for ourselves. Mother's patronizing attitude raised my discomfort level intensely.

Strangely, as I grew older Dad changed. He wasn't the doormat he had been when I was young. He danced attendance on Mother because he truly enjoyed doing things for her and had from the time they first knew one another when they were sweet sixteen. And, with one exception, Mother wasn't the demanding, snooty, demeaning woman of the past. The exception was in her attitude about how I should choose my friends. In fact, she was a vivacious woman who was sought after by people of all ages, races, socio-economic strata, and she wasn't a malingerer. She was really an ill woman who decided to live her life to the fullest as long as she could— and she did. And so I saw that then, we *did* need maids to handle what Mother could not physically handle, and Dad was glad to work hard to see that she had whatever was necessary for her to live as long and happy a life as possible. This revelation made me look at things differently. Following Dad's lead, I did what I could to make Mother's days comfortable and enjoyable. Lest you should think that, in Hollywood fashion, the lights began to dim and the heavens opened up as my revelations dissipated my negative view, not so! They did nothing to dispel my rancor about Mother's interference with my friends, nor did they eliminate my displeasure at having someone do for me the things I could very well do for myself.

As I think back, I realize that my mother did give me my comeuppance in her own inimitable fashion. She certainly knew that her plebian daughter would never become the elegant, fashion-conscious person she had hoped. That had to be why she gave me a lovely set of delicate Venetian ware goblets, champagne glasses and soup bowls, which break from heavy breathing. I learned in a subsequent trip to Italy that they have discontinued that style. The material was too fragile and now can only be seen in the museum (or my house). And that must be why she changed her uncharacteristic refusal to accept the mink coat Dad was determined to get her. This was before the animal rights activists' protests. Knowing of my fierce antipathy to wealth and status symbols, her caveat in taking the mink was that I select it with her because it would be mine after her death. In the fifty-eight years I have had the coat, I haven't worn it a dozen times. Its poshness still makes me uncomfortable— which, if Mother can look down or up or

Mom and dad, 1953

sideways from wherever she is, must give her a chuckle. It did give pleasure to both Dad and Mother at the time.

CHAPTER 8

SEX 101

I got my first menstrual period before noon . . . in school . . . when I was thirteen. I hadn't a clue what all that blood was about, and it scared me to death. It took a longer time than usual to get home for lunch because it's difficult to walk with your legs so tightly together that they feel wrapped around one another. As soon as I entered the house I went to Mother's room, where, as usual, she was on the phone. I stood directly in front of her, pulled down my panties and said, angrily and accusatorily:

"LOOK!"

She looked and laughed! Here I was, dying, and she was laughing!

"I'll have to call you back", she said. "My daughter has just become a woman."

She took me to the bathroom, where she pulled out hidden items—a sanitary belt, sanitary pads, and clean panties. She instructed me to wash myself while she gave her lecture on the "whys" and "wherefores" of the menstrual cycle, including how to use the items she handed me.

I grew older and wiser and more self-assured as I walked back to school. My friends gathered 'round to hear how I'd survived, and they were impressed. None of them had their "periods" yet.

When I got home after school was over, I found a lot of my friends from the neighborhood gathered there, ready to play. Our home was like a clubhouse where everyone felt comfortable and had fun. They weren't lolling around when I got there, but were seated in a circle waiting for Mother to start reading a book she held in her hand. "Being Born" was the textbook for this class. By the time the session was over, we knew about how horses and cattle and dogs and rabbits and the like procreated, but not one useful thing about people, especially not anything about their "sex."

The parents of our visitors thought otherwise. The phone rang off the hook throughout that day and the next with irate parents angrily admonishing mother for having the "audacity" to teach their children about such a subject, which had happened too soon and was their prerogative.

They had the right to select the time and the manner of the telling. They were right, but Mother soldiered on feeling self-righteous and justified, since she hadn't invited their children to her class. She was just teaching her daughter while they listened. That was my mom. I gradually learned about sex as most kids do, from older friends, as well as the chemistry of our bodies, books, movies, and exploration.

Aside: I used the same "textbook" with my kids and added to it.

CHAPTER 9

CIGARETTES

This is how my cigarette smoking began: We were driving through about two feet or more of Buffalo's snow in frigid, one-digit weather on our way to the train station to pick up my friend Barb. I had received a letter from her the day before asking if I would *pu-lease* come to the station with her dad to get her. We had just finished our first year of high school and she wanted to tell me right away about all the exciting things that had happened when she was visiting with her cousin during Christmas vacation. Of course I said yes.

The streets were icy, so we skidded, straightened, slowed, and repeated that pattern many times before arriving at our destination. Even with the heater on, we were freezing so when we got to the train our plan was to enjoy the warmth of the station until Barb arrived. No such luck. Instead, the heating units in the station had all broken down and there was no warmth to be found anywhere. So, our only option was to return to the car where we knew the heater was working. We repeated our very high-stepping—more like leaping—over the even higher snow, back to the car. Once we got in, we turned on the heater and radio. Finally comfortable, we chatted about the snow, the broken heaters, Barb's and my first year in high school, just this and that. Then I suddenly noticed that Barb's dad was inching closer and closer to me until I was glued to the door. Before I could process this, he started groping me. I couldn't push back because he was bigger and stronger than me. If I tried to get away by opening the door—if I could even open it against the snow—where would I go? We were in the middle of nowhere. I was frightened, horrified, and angry. He was the *father* of my girlfriend! I didn't know what to do! In desperation, I asked him for a cigarette. This was my first experience with a cigarette and I hadn't a clue what to do with it. So I puffed away like crazy, didn't cough, choke, gasp, heave, or whatever else I might have done. I *talked* sophisticated and thought the fire of a burning cigarette would be a good safety weapon if used hard, correctly, and on target. I knew I could and would do it. Then I heard a knock on the window behind me and, to my great relief, there was Barb. Fortunately, my safety action wasn't necessary. After she collected her luggage and we did a lot of chatting, I went home.

My friend Betty, who was like a big sister to me, was living with us for the semester while her mother was being treated in the hospital and then rehab. We shared my bedroom and I enjoyed that. When I came in, she asked, as she always did, for the happenings of the day. She became very upset when she heard about Barb's dad's behavior.

"Did you tell your dad?" she asked.

"No, and I'm not telling him. We're talking about Barb's father, for heaven's sake."

"Then I will," said she—and she did.

Dad left the house instantly and said nothing when he returned, but I never saw Barb's dad again. Barb and I still visited one another, but her father was never to be seen when I was at their home. I don't mean to imply that Dad killed him. He was seen by many, but without me.

I questioned Bob about it, wanting to know if Dad had ever spoken to Bob about the whole incident. He hadn't.

And so it began. I liked cigarettes a lot. Smoking was the "in" thing to do. In every movie, the sophisticated people had a drink in one hand and a cigarette in the other, and so, ultimately, did we. 1 smoked them—two packs of Chesterfields a day—they satisfy (so said the ads, and I agreed). So it was more than forty years before I finally stopped cold turkey. Sol, my ex-husband, stopped about two years earlier, apropos of nothing that he ever mentioned. Away went the unfiltered Camels he indulged in—two to three packs a day.

One day when I was sitting in a conference room at the end of a long conference table, I realized I couldn't see the people at the other end of the table because the smoke was so thick. My eyes were running, my throat was burning and hurting something awful. I was not in good shape. I asked myself why I was subjecting myself to such misery and decided I wouldn't do it anymore. That's when I stopped.

I became, instead, an obnoxious reformed smoker. When I'd see a perfect stranger light up, I'd shake my finger in his face and say, "Do you know what you're doing? Do you know you can get cancer from these things? Do you know it can be very painful? Do you know it can *kill* you?!"

It's a wonder one of them didn't get pissed enough to kill *me*, but I'm still hanging around in my very early nineties! Can't say the same for a lot of folks I knew who persisted in smoking like my brother and my Dad and many friends who kicked the bucket before their time. I miss them. We could have enjoyed so many more wonderful days together.

CHAPTER 10

CONFIRMATION DANCE

It was 1934. I was thirteen. It was my first formal dance. I was on top of the world. In reality, I was on the second floor of my house, in my bedroom, pirouetting in front of the mirror, admiring my first evening gown. It was white, floor length, with a sweetheart neckline and a little train that just missed the ground when I wore my matching heels. It was beautiful. Pulling on my long white gloves and draping my short cape over my arm, I lovingly picked up the pretty beaded clutch evening bag my brother had given me. It was just large enough to hold lipstick, a mirror, a small comb, a handkerchief, the house key and the "mad money" we carried in those days (a dime for a phone call in case we had a fight with our dates and had to get a ride home). A last glance in the mirror, and I was ready to make my entrance. I walked carefully down the stairs until I got to the landing, stopped, slowly turned, preened, then

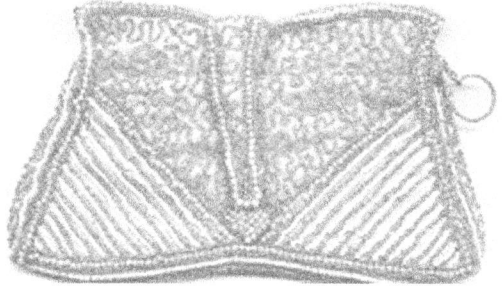

48

theatrically walked the last three steps into the living room—to the "oohs" and "aahs" of my admiring audience: my mother, my father, my brother, and Aunt Mabel's husband, my Uncle Dave. It was incredibly exciting.

Uncle Dave relieved me of my cape and purse and began instructing me on the intricate handling of a train.

Uncle Dave

He modeled for me, gracefully picking up his imaginary train, placing his finger through the little loop then gliding around the room, up the stairs and down. Now, it was my turn. Clumsy at first but improving under his tutelage, I finally mastered it. The final test was holding it while dancing. He modeled again, then became my dance partner. I tried to imitate his smooth performance as we waltzed to the music mother played on the piano, all to the delight of our audience. And then the doorbell rang.

Dad, in his dignified way, opened the door and ushered Elliott into the room. He looked elegant in his dark suit, white shirt, and tie, his hair slicked down—tall, dark and handsome . . . except for the crimson hue that went from his neck to the roots of his hair. He was stressed, but not because of my family, whom he had met many times before. I greeted him, started to tell him how nice he looked, but didn't get the chance. He saw me, walked rigidly forward, holding a floral box stiffly in front of him, thrust it at me and, in a strangled voice said, "Here!" I was thrilled. I accepted it happily, thanked him hurriedly as I tried to open it—and he was relieved. The corsage, my first from a boy (my father had given me one on Valentine's Day), was my favorite, gardenias. I had heard some of my more sophisticated friends talk about orchids, which are lovely but delicate and have no scent. My girlfriends looked at orchids as a status symbol because they were so expensive. That was silly. After a bit of deliberation about where to pin the corsage, mother did the deed, and I felt very special and pretty. A little picture taking, a lot of good wishes and kisses goodbye, all the admonishments parents are compelled to utter, and we were finally ready to leave. Elliott helped me into my cape. With my purse in one hand and my other hand on Elliott's arm, I floated from the house into the waiting car. Our chauffeur was his sweet and discreet sister, Ruth.

We were deposited at Temple, where we made our way to the festively decorated auditorium for the big event. It took no time at all to locate our group, and, in customary fashion, the boys crowded together, and the girls took off to the restroom to make sure every hair was in order, makeup was properly applied, and stocking seams were straight. The mirror got a workout! We were the Belles of the Ball!

Our group had been socializing weekly after Temple services on Friday nights. We took turns going to one home one week, another the next. Our adult chaperones were unobtrusive. The food, soft drinks, and radio or record music was readily available, and avail ourselves we did. We giggled and teased and flirted and danced and gossiped and played parlor games and learned how to enjoy being with one another. We gravitated into couples but never to the exclusion of others. We girls had been nonstop on the phone weeks before the dance, planning, deciding how to dress, comparing our purchases, going over all of the important details in preparation for this superlative event. I suspect the boys burned up the phone wires too, but their details were somewhat different.

When we heard the music begin, we hastily but carefully made our way back to the dance floor and our waiting dates. Elliott and I spent the evening "ballroom" or "close dancing" to the slow music and "jitterbugging" to the fast music (they call it "swing" today) with time out only for some refreshments to re-energize us. It was a wonderful, exciting, romantic night, and we celebrated every second of it until the last strains of "Goodnight Ladies" and "Goodnight Sweetheart" came to an end. Not wanting to break the mood, we softly said our goodbyes and went to our waiting car. Ruth did not intrude, and our ride home was quiet, dreamy. The goodnight kiss was a challenge because, as discreet and invisible as Ruth tried to be, her presence was a deterrent, and the porch light was shining like a 100-watt bulb. A quick, gentle kiss was the best we could bravely manage.

On the other side of the door, my audience waited expectantly, full of questions. I enjoyed recounting the evening's events and probably expanded and inflated them a bit. I carefully removed my gardenias, put droplets of water on them, replaced them in their box, then into the refrigerator to preserve them and show them off as long as possible.

They are gone now, as are the gown and the cape, but the little beaded bag, limp and a bit yellowed with age, still survives, as do the memories of that glorious night, the night of my first formal dance.

CHAPTER 11

FIRST REAL LOVE, MOTHER/DAUGHTER SPLIT

When I was seventeen years old, I met the cousin of a friend of mine. Although he lived in a different city, he visited several times a year for school vacations and for almost the entire summer. His name was Chuck. We started dating and fell in love. We spent as much time together as possible. We went swimming and sunbathing at various spots on Lake Erie and dancing at the two ballrooms nearest to us. We also enjoyed just being together and talking, discussing things that were of interest or importance to us. We became enamored; it was so romantic.

We were very close—my mother felt much too close—so she forbid me to see him anymore. I thought she had no right to tell me how to pick out my friends, especially boyfriends, because I was almost an adult so I should be able to go out with whomever I pleased. My mother said I was to do exactly what she told me since she was the mother, not I, and this was to be the end of the discussion and the end of the dating. She gave notice of this to all relatives but, undaunted, I continued to date Chuck and we continued to be enamored with one another.

One summer day, we were walking on the beach, going to a friend's to have a chat and lunch and a swim, when we passed my aunt's home. I completely forgot she lived there. Without my realizing it, she saw us. Sure enough, she reported us to my mother. My homecoming was horrendous. That's the last I saw of Chuck for years. And the reason for the mother/daughter split. I highly resented Mom's attitude and was never able to be close to her after that.

Throughout the next few years, Chuck and I got little bits of information about each other, but we never saw or spoke to one another again. I later learned he'd graduated from law school and was practicing law. He'd learned I finished my undergraduate degree in preparation for my masters in social work. As time went on, I met and had lots of fun with many folks, and then I met Sol. That's when my whole life changed. It was wonderful. After much loving and talking and loving and dancing and letter writing, we decided to marry.

Then two things happened at once. Chuck became engaged, and Sol and I married. About a month after our wedding, Sol and I visited in Chuck's city. We were going to a dinner party given for us to celebrate our marriage. As we entered the restaurant I saw, to my amazement, Chuck sitting at a table with many friends and much festivity. I went to greet him, and that's when I learned of his wedding. I met his bride very briefly. They married about two weeks before our wedding. My efforts to have Sol meet Chuck failed. A very active, loud, noisy crowd, interested only in getting to their tables quickly, got in our way. That was disappointing. But we couldn't have really talked anyway because each couple was the centerpiece, so to speak, of their dinner party, so they had to be at their own tables quickly. That's the last time I saw Chuck. I still got little bits of information about him until his death many years ago.

As I write this, I find that I'm still unforgiving of my mother and her attitude—thinking she had no right to select my friends and to forbid me from seeing any of them. This has softened a bit by living with five teenage daughters but not enough to really forgive her.

PART TWO

A FEW OF US

CHAPTER 12

LOVE AND MARRIAGE

It was winter vacation during my junior year of college and I was bound for Scranton for fun and games as usual. I was a guest at the home of my long-time friend Dick, whose family I had known since birth. Ray, one of Dick's gang, had invited me to be his date for New Year's Eve. My visits in Scranton and at Ray's parents' cabin in the mountains were always fun. Dick had his girlfriends and I had his

Scranton guys and Sol

boyfriends, a great arrangement for me. Dick and some of his gang interrupted their pinochle game to collect me from the railroad station. It was then I met Sol, an addition to the group. I had never seen or heard of him before, and I might just as well not have for all the attention he paid me. He was handsome, mature, self-assured, and he did not take note of me the way other men did. That was part of his attraction—the challenge of it. They resumed their game while I unpacked and then I joined them. We fell right into our usual good-natured kidding as though I hadn't been gone at all. My date card for the week of merriment was quickly filled, not once by Sol.

Yet he and I were together every day. Sol was never my escort—but he always knew with whom and where I would be. As Mike and I started our dessert course at a local restaurant, Sol appeared, pulled a chair up to our table, and became a major player in our party.

When Jake and I were leaving the movie to go to the local hangout for a snack, there Sol was, joining us as though it were prearranged. And on the very next date, as Buddy and I were selecting balls at the bowling alley, he materialized next to us. My dates were different each day, but wherever I was, Sol was there.

I thought this was serendipity, but I later learned it was by design, his design. I couldn't understand why Sol didn't just ask me out, but I didn't care because we were together, and the others became the outsiders. There was strong chemistry between us from the start. I wanted to be with him. As it happened, he couldn't have afforded to ask me out, but I didn't know that then, so our interactions became suspenseful and all the more enticing. My "official" dates were amazingly tolerant.

We attended the same elaborate New Year's Eve festivities, Sol with his date and me with mine. Almost from the first, we spent more time with one another than with those with whom we came. We danced, we talked, talked and danced—the old-fashioned kind of dancing, close in one another's arms . . . closer and slower. We touched, caressed—we kissed—we electrified one another. The looks, the nearness, even without direct contact, set off sparks—tingling—breathless. On New Year's Eve, our last night, it was hard to pull apart. New Year's Day, our tenth day together, was when I had to leave. The guys boarded the train to give me a warm "hugs-and-kisses" sendoff. Just before I departed for the university with another classmate who'd also visited, Sol gave me a kiss goodbye that shook the very foundation of the universe. As we pulled out of the station, my classmate, who had saved a seat for me and watched the proceedings, asked if the passionate kisser was Ray.

"No," said I. "That was Sol."

"Who?"

"The man I just met and fell in love with. He's a keeper." And so it began.

Sol and I corresponded, a lot. Newsy letters turned into "like" letters that evolved into tentative love letters. Then came graduation, mine from college and Sol's from Officer Candidate School (OCS), since he had enlisted in the army after we parted. I accepted his invitation to graduation at Ft. Belvoir, Virginia. Sol gave me a tour of the army camp—including the barracks, not realizing women weren't allowed there. We worried they might not graduate him because of this, but they did.

The chemistry between us was still there, full blown. We decided to marry—and kidded for a long time about who'd proposed to whom. We alternated back and forth depending upon what we were trying to prove. It didn't matter. We agreed the wedding would be one month later, when Sol would have leave from OCS.

When I phoned to tell my parents the news, Dad—who'd just stepped out of the shower and wrapped himself in a towel—dropped it and yelled for Mother. Her oft-quoted response was:

"Come home at once; you have a dental appointment."

Neither Sol nor I had met or known much about the other's family, and we didn't care—we were in our own cocoon. We knew next to nothing about one another except that being together felt good. I think that was lust. We didn't know one another well enough for it to be love. My parents asked very few questions about Sol, and those were only related to arrangements for the wedding—large or small, formal or informal, his guest list, etc. However, my brother Bob, two years my junior, gave me the third degree:

"Which of the men pictured on your dresser is he?"

"He's not there."

"Is he the guy who gave you his wings?"

"No, that was Buddy."

"How long have you known him?"

"Ten days in person and a year of letter writing."

"What do you know about his family?"

"He supports his mother and sister."

"What are his thoughts on major topics, his aims and goals?"

On and on Bob went. I didn't know and really didn't care.

As the time for the wedding drew closer, I got the jitters. Bob had been right. Sol was really a stranger. I was nervous, apprehensive, fearful of what I was getting into. When he arrived, we were to meet in front of the life-size stuffed buffalo at the train station. It was time. Mother was busy dusting and vacuuming so that the apartment would be presentable for Sol— as if he would notice. I had butterflies. Dad sensed my feelings and asked to drive me to the depot. I heaved a sigh of relief and sophisticatedly acquiesced. When Dad saw a scrawny, older man standing at the buffalo obviously waiting for someone, he asked in a rather pathetic tone of voice if it was Sol. When Sol walked around the corner and Dad saw he was the handsome one in his second Lieutenant's uniform, he was visibly relieved. Sol was also anxious—about meeting the family, going through the ceremonies and rituals—but the feelings we had for one another had not diminished.

We married on July 28, 1943, and the whirlwind began. Sol's mother and sister did not attend the wedding—they "had nothing to wear." My cousin and Sol's Pennsylvania cousins, who represented his family, were our witnesses. We wanted a small wedding, very small and simple. We made it clear, did all but draw diagrams to emphasize our point. We got no argument. That was because no attention was paid to our request. We could have saved our breath. The grand compromise was having

Irma and Sol, the happy couple.

the ceremony in my rabbi's study instead of the chapel or temple proper. The study was packed with so many people the walls bulged. No long white wedding gown

Mother and Dad

and veil like Aunt Jean's years ago. The army uniform for Sol and a street-length dress for me. The rest of the family followed suit in their simple dress; after all, the country was at war. The family dinner and reception in the major hotel was for a mere 350 guests. This was the moderately small and modest wedding my parents thought was seemly in the time of World War II. Although the ceremony had been held in the study, it had all the traditional, typical, expected trappings.

To tell the truth, I was so nervous I don't remember much about it all. One thing I do remember clearly was the wedding gift we received from my kid cousin Don, in his early teens at the time. It was a heavy handful of change saved from his soda-jerking job at the drug store, our

Irma, Don and his car, 1944.

most touching, meaningful, and memorable gift.

I thought Sol was worldly, sophisticated. Boy, was I ever wrong! Our best man, Bernie, became ill at the last minute, and Al, who substituted for him, did a marvelous job. I learned he made reservations for our hotel room because Sol thought we would be returning to my parent's home. Al also informed Sol it was not incumbent upon us to remain at the reception on our wedding night until the last guest left.

My wedding was not the great romantic phenomenon of a young girl's dreams. Sol and I were both too emotionally wrung out. The whole affair felt unreal. It was even more unreal when we ended up taking our best man and maid of honor to breakfast the next morning.

Sol's leave was very short, so there I was, a twenty-one year old bride fresh from the altar, on my way to Port Chester, New York, to meet his family for the first time. Even though Sol did have enough lead time to accompany me, I was scared to death. What was I doing? I knew nothing about his family, nothing about marriage and housekeeping, and, worst of all, practically nothing about Sol. Ten days of being together and a year of letter writing aren't long enough to really know one another. It didn't feel like it, anyhow. Not right then.

But suddenly I was swept up meeting mother, sister, aunts, uncles, and cousins—all very welcoming, so all was right with the world. There was no question that Sol was the "be all and end all" with his mother and sister and ranked very highly with the rest of the family. The days rushed by as we were entertained and hurriedly examined by the relatives in our brief stay in Portchester. Sol was uncomfortable with his mother and sister's fawning but held up well for our short visit.

Soon our time was up, and we dashed to Grand Central to begin our life together, which started rapturously and breathlessly.

CHAPTER 13

SOL: PART I

Sol never knew his father, not even his father's name, although the last name on his birth certificate or

GI Sol

high school diploma was Levine. He used the "L" as his middle initial all his life. No one ever said who Levine was, what he was like, where he was from or where he went. It was a well kept secret, a mystery. There was, of course, a great deal of speculation, both good and evil. I don't know if Sol ever used Levine as a last name, but he ultimately took his stepfather Jake Fisher's name even though he was never legally adopted. Sol never said how he felt about all this. He made a few feeble attempts to question his mother about his biological father but stopped because she cried each time the subject was brought up. I questioned her when I was pregnant with our first child. I persisted even though she was crying. She said he was handsome, charming, had no health problems and that was all I got from her. The way she said it, however, told me she had loved him.

Pa was the only father Sol knew, and he was very fond of him.

Ma, Esther Muffs Fisher, lived with her brother when she came from Lithuania to the land of milk and honey at age eighteen. She worked as a highly skilled corset seamstress to contribute to the household. There was a big, gaping hole between her exhaustive and enthusiastic

Ma, at age 18.

account of life in Lithuania and her life in the States before the birth of her son. She was one of 12 children, from her father's second wife. She was devotedly attached to her father, a remarkable man who chose to return to Lithuania after having run away to escape conscription in the army. He returned in order to smuggle Jews, who suffered regularly from Pogroms, out of the country. He did it successfully with such ploys as dressing the men in women's clothes so they could make it across the borders. She did not leave the country until after his death.

One would think her life in the States did not begin until Sol was born. She doted on him and worked long and hard hours to support him. He was in a day and night nursery when she was away from home, then in day care, then in regular school.

Sol was eight or nine when his mother married Pa. They came from the same village in Lithuania. They met in New York City when they were both greenhorns. Pa was frequently hospitalized after having been gassed in World War I, so he was never able to make a decent living in his candy

Sol and Ma

store or his fish market. After having a second child, a daughter, when Sol was ten, Ma continued to work. They were on welfare during the Depression and Pa had a newsstand. When Sol was in high school and helped out at the stand, he discovered that Pa was acting as a bookie to make extra money. Pa would instruct Sol as to how to respond to phone calls when he wasn't there. This side business came to a sudden halt when Ma found out. They were living in Chicago at the time.

In the summer, Sol worked at the Civilian Conservation Corps, one of Roosevelt's alphabet organizations. He completed a two-year high school course for children who couldn't complete four years to get a diploma because they had to work. He was valedictorian of his class. The boys wore white jackets, black pants, and black shoes to graduation. He had no black shoes, and

Civilian Conservation Corps

there was no money for them. He never got over the embarrassment he felt when he had to appear on the podium in front of everyone in his sneakers.

Pa contracted tuberculosis during one of his hospitalizations and remained institutionalized for twenty years, going from one hospital to another and finally to a TB sanitarium in upper New York state. I first met him after all my children were born. I fully expected a shut-in of that length of time to be cantankerous, surly, generally unpleasant. I was wrong. TB had stricken so many of his bones that it was hard for him to sit up, yet before we came, he conned a new attendant into putting him in a wheelchair as though it were his regular routine. It wasn't. Although he had been completely bedridden, he kept current on everything that was going on in the world. He avidly read the newspapers projected on the ceiling of his room and followed the clothing and other ads. A mystery fan, he read all the latest books.

He wanted to see his grandchildren, and the doctor gave permission as long as he never kissed or hugged them or was in a confined area with them. We were told his TB was arrested but could flare up again in a moment, which would put the children at risk.

He made the trip to Buffalo by train with an attendant. The first thing he requested upon his arrival was to be taken to a men's clothing store so he could outfit himself in up-to-date clothes. Now he could meet his grandchildren, who were nursery and grade-school age. It was summer, so we picnicked outdoors and played. He stayed in a nursing home with a winding staircase and no elevator. Sol carried him, wheelchair and all, up and down it several times each day. Pa thoroughly enjoyed his visit, and so did we. He died shortly after his return to the sanitarium, his mission accomplished.

When Sol was sixteen, Ma sent him to live with an uncle in Port Chester, New York, because he was in with a very bad crowd in Chicago. She was sure they would end up in prison or dead and, for the most part, she was right. Healthy, gregarious Sol was popular, particularly with the girls. It was easy enough for him to meet them, since the uncle with whom he'd first lived had four daughters. His patter was such that you would think he'd swallowed the blarney stone. No one suspected he was underage when he got a job parking cars because he looked older than his years, so they never asked to see his driver's license.

He moved from one uncle to another and ended in the home of an aunt in Scranton, Pennsylvania. She endeared herself to me on our first meeting, when I was a bride. She, the mother of one, said for the world to hear, in a voice filled with disdain and in my presence, "Look at her. She's so scrawny she'll never be able to have children." The unsubtle implication being that Sol shouldn't waste his time on this inadequate nothing.

Sol worked in her son-in-law's pants factory. He was an energetic, responsible and loyal worker but naive in business matters. He felt inordinately grateful when his cousin helped to pay for his appendectomy. It never occurred to him that he was being underpaid for the job. He gradually got an apartment for himself and his mother and sister and provided for them until his sister married and his mother died.

Although he would not be conscripted to serve in the military in World War II because he had two dependents, his mother and sister, he enlisted in the army and went to Officer's Candidate School to become an officer. He entered the service in part due to patriotism, in part to have the government to pay for his dependents, and for the most part to get out into the world—away from all his responsibilities. And then, he turned around and married me, and we made a family.

CHAPTER 14

WORLD WAR II:

WHEN THE YANKS INVADED THE SOUTH

We sprinted, suitcases in hand, to catch our train at Grand Central—no porters during wartime. Had to get going so Sol could be in camp on time. Had to go into the great unknown, to his army post in Kentucky. I was anxious, apprehensive. We gaspingly got to the gate just as it was closing—in time to see our train pull out without us. A short wait, then caught a ride on the brand-new 20th Century Limited. We were lucky—such luxury—a cool, clean, quiet, smooth ride. That was more like it. A real honeymoon.

Then Chicago to Evanston. A tiny, bare-essentials hotel room and it was hot— very hot—and the fan blew directly on us but gave no relief. Then the train for Henderson, Kentucky, and what a let-down—what a contrast to that streamlined, posh transport we'd left the day before. A steam engine, an old clunker, clanging and bumping its way down south, windows open, soot blowing and covering everything and everybody. Service men, wives, and camp followers crowded together filling all seats, sitting on suitcases in the aisles, sweaty, hot, cramped, miserable. The noise, the swaying back and forth colliding into one another, the polluted air, and the interminable length of time it was taking to get there. Could hardly wait.

Finally arrived. Where to go? Didn't think of that in advance. Sol would go back to camp, but what about me? There were no quarters there for me. Had to find a place, and fast, because Sol had to return to his barracks by a set time. Had to knock on doors and find rooms to rent. The places were filled up and it was hard to impossible to get suggestions on other likely places.

Tired, hot, desperate, and hungry, we then saw a movie-set-stereotypical haunted house. It was way back from the sidewalk, with overgrown weeds almost waist high, a frame structure in ill repair, broken wooden shutters, and a sagging front porch, decidedly uninviting—nothing like the lovely Southern plantation homes we saw in the movies and books—but we had to try it. The apparition who slowly, reluctantly opened the door must have been Methuselah's wife—frail, incredibly wrinkled, ghostly pale, paper-thin skin, claw-like hands. In a dry voice, she made it plain that she hated this war (her sons left to serve in it), she hated women, and she hated

the "godamnedyankees"—*but* she needed money—so we could rent a room with only breakfast kitchen privileges.

The room, a bedroom— large, high ceilinged, double bed as centerpiece, wardrobe against one wall, bare yellow-coated 40-watt bulb hanging from a long wire over the middle of the bed.

Irma and Sol in Henderson, Kentucky.

Not appealing. Not welcoming. Sol placed my suitcase on the floor of "our room" with a quick kiss goodbye and a promise to come back soon— not sure when. He beat a hasty retreat to his comfortable quarters. I stayed—alone—and frightened.

Barely surviving the night, I later walked the few short blocks to a small grocery store in the town square. I purchased my few supplies—bread for toast, oranges, cereal, milk, a stick of butter, and small boxes of tea and sugar. The townspeople stared at me—not a single friendly "hello"—and the servicemen hooted, made unpleasant sounds and advances. Eyes straight ahead, I hurried back to my room. The harridan, just as unpleasant as she was the day before, grudgingly showed me where to find dishes, glasses, silverware, bread box, etc., then left. After much difficulty holding onto the flatware—it slithered out of my hands—I made my tea, sliced my orange, poured out my cereal, opted to eat bread and butter, no toast—not after seeing the filth-encrusted toaster—and gingerly ate my breakfast. Tomorrow I would get cleaning supplies—soap to wash whatever dishes, glasses, and utensils I needed to use.

I would have liked to explore the area, even in the heat, if the people had been friendly or I hadn't been alone. What had happened to that Southern hospitality I'd heard so much about? It was not to be seen, heard or felt. When Sol got back, and he would sometime soon, we would case the joint.

Today was better. Nothing like a good night's sleep to restore the spirits. Solved the mystery of the slippery silverware. After watching my witch landlady cook up an incredibly greasy mess of stuff, I saw her "clean"—that's a laugh—her flatware. It never was touched by soap or even water but was wiped off with—of all things—wax paper! Then, as I took my freshly bought bread out of the breadbox, I found the rats had beaten me to it, leaving their little teeth marks as evidence. That did it! All meals and as much time as possible would be spent out of this house. Thank goodness, only here for four weeks. I could handle that. Then on to Tennessee. I would find the real beautiful South there.

A first was my introduction to military life—the Corps of Engineers of the 98th Division—the northern division that invaded the South, or so the Southerners felt. The colonel and some of the other officers were "regular army," which they took very seriously and competitively. They looked down on the "90-Day Wonders" who went through and became instant officers. They were anxious to get "into action" (into combat) because that made the likelihood of promotion greater. Thank heavens my husband wasn't one of these people.

Then came another first: tea with the other officers' wives at the Colonel's house. Stiff and formal. I was at the bottom of the totem pole, since my husband was a lowly second lieutenant. This was decidedly not the life for me. I was turned off by the viciousness of the wives pulling their husband's ranks on one another. There was no feeling of unity or camaraderie. It had to get better than this.

Next stop Lebanon, Tennessee—maneuvers. We women preceded our men, spending one night in Nashville—a lovely city—before house hunting. Learned about those beautiful fireplaces in each room. They warmed only the part of you facing them, leaving the rest of you shivering and cringing. Had to keep turning, like on a spit, to get any benefit. Got caught up in a convoy on our ride to Lebanon. Saw our husbands but couldn't communicate with them. Frustrating. We didn't know where we were going, hadn't found our quarters yet. The men knew our hotel in Nashville, so they used it as our message center until we could connect.

I joined two newfound friends, and together we located a couple who, for the first time, were renting rooms in their single-family home. The man had experienced a heart attack, could no longer work and needed the money. Our husbands could only join us on the weekends, so we had minimal time together as couples, but we women had long hours to get to know our landlords and their ways. We had kitchen privileges for breakfast—this time in a clean kitchen with food we supplied ourselves—at least at the start. I, the Jewish wife, put my leftover breakfast tomato juice in a glass in the refrigerator. I later learned this terrified my landlords, who had just discovered their first tenants were a Protestant

Ham and Dot, WASPS

Sol and Irma, Jewish

Helen and Joe, Catholic

couple, a Catholic couple, and a Jewish couple. They thought the red liquid was the blood of children—wasn't that what Jews drank? Their prejudices against Catholics, Jews, and negroes (as they were politely called) were flagrant. These were the days of separate drinking fountains—"colored," white—and separate everything else.

This family had been in the community, and in a seeming time warp, for generations. The landlord's

Surrey

mother looked like a character from Dickens, with the black velvet ribbon at her neck, sleeves to her wrists, a skirt to her ankles, and high-button shoes. She drove about in a horse-drawn surrey and had many parlors in her house, the walls of each adorned with photographs of ancestors in shadow-box frames.

Overall our "innkeepers" were kind to us—just happening to have chicken dinner 'leftovers" when our men were home on the weekends— enough to feed the six of us, although they themselves were only two. They acted as gracious hosts, so it was appalling when

Our gracious landlords

the family album revealed a picture of the landlord and many of the townsmen, whom we had come to recognize, standing around a tree in the town square—from which a black man was hanging by the neck—dead! There were smiles on the faces of the people in the photograph—and every face stood out in bold relief! It was a horror.

In direct contrast was the behavior of the landlady, who tended an ill, bedridden, elderly black woman in the black part of town. The landlady bathed her, fed her, cleaned her house, scrubbed her floor, attended to her every want, made her as comfortable as possible. If I had not seen this with my own eyes, I wouldn't have believed it. For long hours in the days that followed, my discussions with my fellow tenants centered upon this dichotomy. The possible explanation that the elderly lady was a "white nigger" did nothing to dispel the abhorrence we all felt. Arguments, impassioned speeches did not change the thinking or attitudes on either side.

Maneuvers complete, the next stop was Camp Rucker in Ozark, Alabama—a town that didn't make the map until the 98th Division invaded it. I agreed to drive a lieutenant's car to the new post. It would save us money and help him out. I drove alone through Birmingham and Montgomery with no place to stay, no hotel reservations. The Air Force graduation filled the towns, and there wasn't a room to be found. It was night—I hadn't had dinner—had to locate something. Through the yellow pages, I found a room at a Hotel Roosevelt, selected because the name itself was comforting and, because of FDR, it gave a feeling of protection. I located the place with some difficulty.

The building was squeezed between rows of bars. The lobby was long and narrow, lined with spittoons, torn black upholstered couches—and men. It felt like a mile, maybe more, from the door to the desk, and double that distance up the stairs (no elevator) to my room on the third floor. The bed

Home in Ozark , Alabama

was made, after a fashion, and empty liquor bottles were everywhere. The bathroom was "down the hall." The only friendly, trustworthy person was the "colored" porter who escorted me to an eatery a few doors away and watched for me when I made my way back. He must have recognized the terror I felt.

There were no locks on the two doors, one to the hall from my bedroom and another to an adjoining room. To get as far away as possible from the filth and the roaches, I remained fully clothed, put my suitcases on the bed, climbed on top of them and waited for the dawn, when I could leave, never once closing my eyes.

In Ozark I fought, almost literally, for a one-room apartment (so called). It had been a store but was divided into two inadequate dwellings. Ours was the storefront, with the window from ceiling to floor and wall to wall, which couldn't be opened because it was right on the street. That was our all-purpose room containing the double bed and the pot-bellied coal stove. Our steamer trunk acted as our wardrobe and chest of drawers. The hallway, extending from the multipurpose front area to the back of the small apartment, had two rooms off it, the kitchen and the bathroom. The kitchen, the largest room, held a table with two chairs, a sink, an icebox, and a three-burner oil stove with a box for an oven. One burner didn't work at all, the second almost touched the ceiling, and the third couldn't boil water. Neither of us knew how to bank a fire in the coal stove to prevent being overcome by its lethal fumes. So the safest heating was steam from the hot water in the bathroom and the flames from the oil stove. The most effective and enjoyable way of keeping warm was body heat from our coupling.

It was Alabama's coldest winter in fifty years. The snow stayed on the ground, to the delight of the northerners, who made snowmen, threw snowballs, and enthusiastically cavorted in the beautiful white stuff. The dampness, however, was palpable even indoors, as it came through the cement walls. Coal was rationed and went to the townsfolk

Irma with coal rations.

first. I purchased it at the railroad siding if I could get the town's one taxi early enough to be close to the head of the line for a hundred-pound sack, one to a customer. The cab driver was so independent that he remained seated and left the customer struggling to heft the sack into the trunk of his car. Kindling wood and ice were sold by a man whose skin was covered with running lesions. He was notorious for literally chasing after the women. My common-wall neighbor was also an army wife. She and I worked out a tapping code to alert one another when he approached, to avoid any end runs around the kitchen table when he made his deliveries.

I knew nothing of cooking, cleaning, or housekeeping. Sol never saw the first meal I prepared in Ozark on our three-burner oil stove. The chicken went from the oven directly to the trashcan, with all its innards still inside. (The chicken I had been used to seeing my mother prepare had already been cleaned out by the butcher and, if I gave it any thought at all, that was how I expected it would always be at the time of purchase. I hadn't a clue that only the chicken's feathers had been removed at that time, the insides completely intact.)

Entertainment consisted of going to one movie theater that showed only Ma & Pa Kettle, and that just on the weekends.

Our other diversion was walking through the cemetery, looking at the raised graves and counting the number of infant deaths. The townspeople were unpleasant, and some were downright unfriendly—like the one dentist in town. He spent his days sitting on his stoop, shooting at squirrels. When he tore himself away to tend to my infected cavity that resulted from the extraction of my wisdom tooth, he shot ice water into the hole. He got back at one Yankee!

During the nine months of going from army camp to army camp, Sol and I began very tentatively to get to know one another. We shared the facts, but not our feelings. Sol hadn't a clue about my fears and trepidation as I tried to cope with the major changes of marriage, military life, and living in the South—the triple whammy. I was uneasy about the first part, and absolutely detested the other two. I was an alien in a land full of senseless taboos. Sol liked the regimentation of army life, commanding a platoon of men, the physical demands of the obstacle courses and hikes. He had no problem with the hierarchy of the military, with taking orders or giving them. He enjoyed being an officer, even though he began in the lowest rank. He was comfortable and insulated with his buddies in the camps, where the routine remained the same. His Northern Division stayed northern, even though they relocated. I hated the protocol of the army, the bigotry and disregard for life that I witnessed in the Southerners.

The traditional "Southern hospitality" that was touted in books, movies, and plays was pure fiction. We were persona non grata. I was a displaced person—always in the wrong place—used the "colored" drinking fountain instead of the "white" one, entered the NCO club because it looked like fun, only to be told I couldn't remain because my husband was an officer. Sol and I rarely discussed our differences pertaining to these things.

Then one day, I interrupted Sol's interminable occupation with his Engineer Corps outfit—putting up and taking down the Bailey Bridge. I was anxious to tell him that the doctor confirmed what we hoped was true: I was pregnant. Almost all the wives were "that way" before our husbands were shipped out. It insured our immortality at a time when none of us knew what tomorrow would bring in a war-torn world. There was a virtual parade to the office of the OB/GYN on the base. The all-pervading mantra was: "I'm in my third/fifth/seventh month—can I travel?" Of course, the answer was always "yes." We all knew we were going to leave for home regardless.

"Don't overdo it, get enough rest, take your time." We all did. Time was something we had plenty of, with our men gone.

And finally, my military stint was over—except for the waiting—and I escaped back to the civilization of the North, where bigotry was so covert that I didn't realize until later that it truly existed even there. I did try to follow Sol to Hawaii after viewing pictures of him basking on the beach while I was strenuously pushing the baby carriage through the deep snow of Buffalo. The Second Service Command said they supposed the baby and I could go—no one had ever asked that question before. It was only after baby Scott and I got our shots in preparation for our trip that they called back to say "no," not even the permanent residents were allowed back at this time. It was hard to accept that I could follow him to the hellholes of the South and not to the beautiful, luxurious islands of Hawaii. But the citizens of Ozark had probably celebrated as us "goddamnedyankees" pulled out. And I never whistled Dixie or stood reverently with my hand over my heart when it was played. Our son was

Sol at beach in Hawaii.

more than two years old when Sol finally returned home, and that's when we first began to establish a real married life—this time with a family—and I even learned to cook.

CHAPTER 15

BROTHER BOB: PART II

When the war was over, Bob and his friend, Moish, decided to take advantage of the G.I. Bill by going to school somewhere out of the country. They considered England and France but decided on Palestine, close to the end of the British Mandate there. They attended Hebrew University for a few months until the British pulled out and the War for Independence began. Then the Arabs closed the road to the university and Bobby had to decide whether to return to the United States or stay there. If he stayed, it would be to fight. That's what he did. He became an officer, fought in the siege on Jerusalem and was badly injured in that fray. He was paralyzed from the waist down for about six months and had a very slow recovery. He met his wife Ofra there, a Sabra (native

Bob and Ofra

Israeli) and an officer in the army. After his marriage, he visited the States often but never returned to live here.

He became a dyed-in-the-wool Israeli, a Jerusalemite, and remained in Israel even while he

Sons: Ron, Don, Gil, 1985

agonized when his three sons had to fight in the various wars. It pained him to see them in danger when he could not replace them or take an active part in the military. The residual effect of his injury, along with his age, precluded that. Instead, he worked in a bakery to fill in for men who were in the service. His sons chided him, saying his efforts there aided the Arabs more than the Israelis.

He worked obsessively for men who were disabled, paraplegic and quadriplegic, helping them in every way possible. He made concerted efforts at fundraising for sorely needed equipment both in Israel and in the States. It was not unexpected for Bob to channel his energies in that direction. It was consistent with the work he'd done at the Crippled Children's Hospital when he was in high school. However, it was a poor choice for him at the time—providing a constant reminder of what could happen to his boys, who were in the throes of battle. Each time a new group of wounded came in, he looked with dread for his sons. He had to give this work up after a while because it drained his nerves and physical well-being.

Bob and Moish opened the first Laundromat in the State of Israel. The venture was short lived … they had to go out of business when they were unable to get soap. Next, they tried selling kerosene

Moish and Bob

stoves, which was not very lucrative. They ultimately returned to school. Bobby became a professor of English literature; he helped establish the English Department at the Hebrew University and was instrumental in establishing the English Dept. at the University of Tel Aviv. He taught there until he retired. He was a respected and loved teacher, according to his students.

I observed Bobby in the classroom where he made his specialty, nineteenth-century literature, come alive. I

Prof. Bobby at
University of Tel Aviv.

marveled that he could remain so enthusiastic about it, keeping it fresh, through all the years he taught. I knew that the complimentary things I was hearing about Bobby as a teacher could have just been fashioned for me, because I was his sister. Then I met a young woman who dispelled these doubts. I was on a tour in England, and she was traveling with her young daughter. I overheard them speaking Hebrew and inquired as to whether they were Israeli. I learned they lived in Tel Aviv, and the woman attended the university there. I asked if she had taken English literature; she said she had, but she didn't know Professor Reisman or Reuven Reisman (as he was formally known in Israel). Then she told me her professor, who was marvelous, the best teacher she ever had, was named Bobby. It was then I learned my brother was "Bobby" to one and all—his children, his friends and his students. Teaching was what he loved. Opposed to the "publish or perish" attitude of universities, he published only his doctoral thesis, and that simply because he had to. Others published books *about* him, but Bob published nothing else.

He was a wonderful father, good with children—once they were able to speak—frightened of them before that. His wife had a kindergarten on the premises where they lived, and he began making wood carvings to entertain the youngsters (especially a certain latch-key child in Bob's charge). He started with totems, then made heads out of avocado pits, graduating to carving beautiful nudes of women and men and some fanciful creatures. He ultimately made life-size statues of people and positioned them permanently in his magnificent garden. He loved the

good earth and had a garden of the biggest, most diversified and breathtakingly beautiful roses I've ever seen. He took great pride in it, and in his statuary.

Rose garden

These were his escape valves, which were much needed.

Bobby was an intense, deeply caring person with a delightful sense of humor. Gregarious, he made friends easily and kept them. Once, when I notified him that Mother was exceedingly ill, he "hitchhiked" all the way from Israel to Buffalo, New York. He had no cash (the banks weren't open), but he was able to borrow money from long-time friends spanning a number of countries, and he made the trip in an amazingly short time.

He taught his Israeli friends about America, with an emphasis on Western movies. I don't think there was a John Wayne or other Western they did not see—many, many times—which he knew because he tested them on the films' contents.

It wasn't until 1985 that I was able to make my first trip to Israel. The expense and responsibility of children and work, as well as Sol being nervous about my being so far from him, combined to delay the journey. It was exciting to know I would at last see my brother in his own home, with his family around him and at his place of

work. My Israel experience began, on our way to his home from the airport, with a flat tire on the slope of the Kahstehl, with crazy drivers speeding by. Bob was excited to finally show me his new country, and I don't think he left out a grain of sand or a blade of grass in his tours and descriptions. He felt he had to do this all

Flat tire on the Kahstehl.

at once in case I never returned.

What made the biggest impact on me then—and in subsequent visits I *did* make—was the size of the land. Israel is so very small a country. My brother lived in

Jerusalem but commuted to Tel Aviv daily. I thought that must be very demanding until I learned that the distance was only about forty-five miles. My sister-in-law's first visit to the States was to our home in Buffalo. She told me she had a good friend she'd like to see and asked if we could drop in for a little while on Saturday. I asked where her friend lived. It was in California.

At home, when I had time to read the log I'd kept so carefully of my time in Israel, I gradually absorbed where I'd been and what I'd seen. It was as overwhelming as Bob's enthusiasm. I need no prompts, however, to remember where I ate the sweetest, most tender, delicious lobster—of all things—that I've ever tasted. Lobster, decidedly not kosher—in Israel? Yes, in Acco . . . and my mouth still waters at the thought of it.

Lobster in Acco!?

While visiting Eilat, a lovely vacation spot, you could see the heavy smoke coming out of the smoke stacks in Jordan, and the people walking around. When you looked in the other direction, where a sign was pointing, it showed the few miles we were from Egypt. I had wanted to go to Egypt to see the pyramids and other legendary things, but the country wouldn't let me in because my passport was only for Israel. If I had gone to Egypt and *then* to Israel, however, I would have been able to visit both places.

On one of my early trips, we were taking a drive so I could see more of the country. The first thing I remember is the phone call that was made to find out the safest route to travel. In the States such a phone call would have been to ask for a weather report. But I learned this call was different when later, as we were driving down a very narrow, one-car-at-a-time street, I heard my brother and Moish asking one another quietly if they had ever been on this road before and if they knew where it would end. The concern in their voices was palpable. The land we were on was flat and we were surrounded by breathtakingly beautiful wildflowers, so I asked why they didn't just make a U turn and retrace our steps.

"Because the land is mined, Irma." That's also when I learned that Syria was only a short distance from there. Life is very different in Syria.

On my next to last trip to Israel, Bob had developed an annoying habit of tapping his fingers on various surfaces. I should have realized its significance much sooner than I did. He had finally grown fingernails, having overcome his lifelong habit of chewing them down

Bob with his usual cigarette.

to the quick. Unfortunately, he didn't do the same with chain-smoking. When I returned home, I decided to phone him to ask how he liked being a bachelor again. All his family was going out of town in different directions, and he was home alone. It took several times before I reached someone on his phone, and it wasn't Bob but a friend of one of his sons. Bob was suffering with a migraine headache the doctors couldn't ease. I knew it was something more serious. He'd suffered from migraines for years and this was not how they affected him. I called the airlines and booked passage back to Israel. I'd been right. He had cancer.

I stayed in Bob's home, per his request, and I'm glad I did. Ofra had the philosophy that taking pain medication and staying in bed or in a hospital or hospice showed weakness, and that was unacceptable to her. She withheld his pain meds, which I didn't know because her talks with the doctor were always in Hebrew, a language I didn't understand. I only later learned about Ofra's doings, when I overheard Bob in his weak and angry voice that brooked no nonsense telling her she was to give him his medications or he would go to the hospital. I was furious. I walked to the home of Ofra's very close friend and told her what was happening. She phoned Ofra and ended up yelling at her, furiously. The doctor had told Ofra that Bob could go to hospice several weeks ago, and she hadn't told him. I did. Then he called her over to him in his weak but firm voice, ordered her to tell the doctor he wanted to go to hospice right away, and asked me to promise not to leave until he died—and he was in hospice that day.

He died three months later of cancer, which began in his lungs and spread quickly throughout his body. Since he knew he was dying, he wanted only to be as comfortable as possible and to enjoy, as best he could, the time he had left. And he did. In addition to family, a virtual parade of friends and students visited him until almost the very end. Bob sat in the lotus position on his sickbed, with his no-hair Yul Bryner look, and pontificated to the audience at his feet. When he was too weak to continue his talks, he lost himself in his music, alternating between classics and the oldies—big bands, Billie Holiday, Mills Brothers, Ella Fitzgerald, and more.

In spite of the years we'd lived so far apart, Bob and I had remained close. Our visits never lasted less than a month at a time, and they generally happened two or three times a year. In between we phoned back and forth about every other week. We talked non-stop and never ran out of topics interesting to us both. I was very fortunate to be able to spend every day of Bob's last three months with him. One of the things he told me during those months was that he'd had a full life and did everything he wanted to do. The only regret he had is that he had no grandchildren.

Even though he died in 1988, I still find myself reaching for the phone to share a happening with him. He did have the good grace before he died to apologize for predeceasing me. But . . . that's not at all what a kid brother should do.

He gave the bulk of his extensive library to the English Department of the University of Tel Aviv, and, a year after his death, his colleagues paid a lovely tribute to him, which my nephew videotaped and shared with me. If I travel to Israel again, I'd like to see the plaque and the part of the library dedicated to him. Bobby fit the definition of a Renaissance man. He was a loving brother, and I miss him.

PART THREE

ALL OF US

CHAPTER 16

HOW YOU CAME TO BE:
AN EXPLANATION WITHOUT APOLOGY

Children have been asked throughout the ages

The very same question by fools and sages:

"What, my son, do you want to be

When you become as old as me?"

It was worded this way for the sons, you see,

It was worded for daughters differently

Because only a "he" was expected to "be"

Whereas "she" was not, being only a "she."

It was pre-ordained, the life of a "she."

It was marriage and raising a family.

With this in mind, in the zeal of youth,

I observed and explored in my quest for the truth.

Having only one sib, I longed for some more.

How much was enough, was it twelve, twenty-four?

The preferred amount at this time was a laugh,

For each mom and dad it was two-and-a-half.

As for gender, no question, I knew without fail

Not a girl in the lot, all the kids would be male.

At the age of thirteen my life's plan was all set:

Marriage, six boys, all conditions were met.

Why no girls, you may ask? It was no surprise.

Their screechy voices brought tears to my eyes,

They tattle, they primp, bat their eyes at the boys,

Have fluff in their heads and keep dolls as their toys.

They leave curlers and makeup all over the place.

The only clean thing they have is their face.

I forgot Mother Nature was also a girl

Til she pointed it out with one heck of a whirl.

"You presume too much," she said with a blast

Your first boy child will be your last!"

And true to her word, that's the way it went,

As the boy child, Scott, would often lament.

Along came Jo, Toby, Di, Sue and Debbie

And nowhere is there a more marvelous bevy

Of children than these despite the gender.

I'm delighted with what we finally did render.

JoAnn

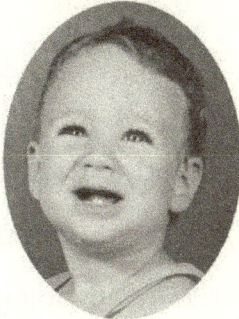

Debbie

Toby

Scott

Susan

Diane

CHAPTER 17

THAT'S MY BOY!

"A healthy, inquisitive nature, you say! You're laughing. You think it's funny. You take him until he's eighteen and then give him back!" I couldn't believe it. He was supposed to be taking a nap in Mother's bedroom while we were chatting. It was nearing our appointment time with the pediatrician. As I went down the hallway, a bouquet of fragrance second to none overtook me. The sight I beheld when I entered the room was utterly incredible! Perfumes, cologne, hand creams, face creams, nail polish were all together in a colorful, odiferous mix, and the creator was finger-painting with it as far as his little arms and hands could reach. He had decorated the bedspread, the dresser, the crib, the crib mattress, and most of all, himself. With a beautiful, angelic smile he spread out his arms to show me the wondrous things he had wrought. Mother thought it was cute. Are all grandparents demented? I had little time for the clean-up and hardly knew where to begin. After a whirlwind of activity with soaps, furniture polish, spot removers, cloths, brushes, and polish remover, it was as good as it was going to get. There were still telltale signs of nail polish on the baby, especially under fingernails and in the navel. Time ran out and there we were, in Dr. Arnold's office, and he was chuckling at the sight of the distraught mother and adorned child.

He never laughed at me when I called about significant *or* insignificant things. When I told him I had

sterilized everything that went in the baby's mouth but that he was chewing the side of his buggy— "What should I do?"—he answered as though my question had merit. I decided he didn't really appreciate the onerous responsibility I had trying to keep this active child alive

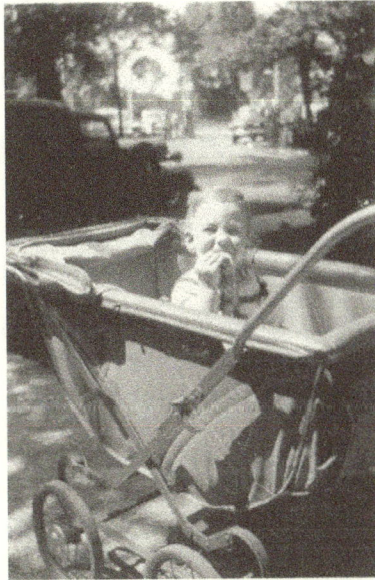

Scott, with who knows what in his mouth.

until his father came home from overseas to meet him.

If Child Protective Services had been in effect in those days, he wouldn't have been home to greet his father. He would have been in a foster home. How many babies have burned the palms of their hands at age nine months, not once, but twice, when in the company of protecting and caring adults? The first time was when he was learning to stand. He pulled himself up holding on to the stove, stood there frozen to the spot, while we admired his prowess. Only when he slid down crying heartbreaking sobs did we realize the insulation of the oven door was far from code. His palms blistered horribly. When they were almost healed, he swung around in his stroller, quick as lightening, and grabbed the hot water pipe. There it was—all over again.

But Dr. Arnold was right. He was a healthy, inquisitive, and active child. Before the days of the Kiddie Koop, Sol contrived a device made of soft chicken wire and rope that encased the entire crib and fastened underneath. Without leaving a clue as to how he did it and no matter how carefully and tightly Sol secured it, Scott was able to get out! It was an act Houdini would have envied. Scott would help himself to food from the refrigerator, then go out the front door in the middle of the night for a walk. We had to put locks high on the doors to the outside to keep him in. They were so high that even I could only reach them when I was on tiptoe. But Scott quickly became adept at piling chairs, books, or whatever else was available—one on top of the other—so that he could climb and reach nearly everything.

His other exploits included turning on all the gas jets of our stove and leaving the house while I was nursing JoAnn. How do you explain to a child the danger of gas when it can't be seen? This, when the pressure was so low that the pilot lights didn't come on automatically. The very day after he turned on the gas jets, the gas stove went out and the electric stove came in!

Then there was the time he happily showed us some slats and part of a railing he'd pulled off the floor of

Scott and Reggie

the back porch that supported the one upstairs. All of this with things from his *toy tool* chest! When I would say, "No, don't touch", it was a signal that he must. Our friendly co-owner of the house would say "no" to her daughter, two days younger than Scott, and Reggie wouldn't even touch the expensive, inviting, fragile porcelain items at ground level in their cabinet. What a relief when the reverse was true with the advent of the second children—our daughter and their son.

Scott was entranced with mechanical toys and learned how to work them very quickly—and then how to take them apart. He only learned how to put them together when he was older and moved out of the house. But he had ideas of how to fix things. One day he came in the house sobbing and full of blood. He'd tripped over his shoelace while running in the driveway and got a big gash under his chin. As I was cleaning him up to assess the damage, he tremulously asked me to get the scotch tape, which would fix it. After more thought, he instructed me to take him to Dr. Arnold's. *He* would fix it. And I did, and he did!

Scott was enterprising. Very early on he contrived a control panel in his bedroom with which he could open and close his door, work his light and radio from his bed. We entered to clean his room with trepidation. It was as though it was booby-trapped. Perhaps it was. Years after he moved out of the house his sisters still asked permission to go into "his" room. They never asked permission to go into "our" room.

He was enamored with clocks, wire recorders,

Scott atop the computer at work.

record players, radios and such, and he continues to be. He has an amazing amount of electronic equipment in his house on which to play his vast collection of old radio shows, movies and music on tapes, CDs, and DVDs with surround sound. He also has a marvelous and varied collection of books in print and on tape. If I should ever be snowed in for an extended period of time, I would want it to be at Scott's with his marvelous aggregation of food for the soul. I would bring my own food for the body because our tastes are different in that department and his oven is the only one I ever saw in which the only dirt was dust. His work is with computers, and he challenged me to learn to use them. He has programmed me so patiently and well that people marvel at what this

old lady is able to do. My beautiful, lively boy has grown into a handsome, inquisitive man who now *can* and *does* fix almost everything.

CHAPTER 18

DADDY'S GIRL

We could hear him stamping the snow off his boots as he came in the house. It was a typical Buffalo, New York, winter with the snow so high it hid the fire hydrants. For the seventh day in a row, he shoveled our long, long driveway from curb to garage to be sure nothing would interfere with the big event. Mother came to stay with two-year-old Scott. Sol was excited. The time for our second delivery was near, and it would be his first experience with the birthing process.

I awakened him in the middle of the night to tell him my water broke. I'd always had dry births. I was freezing, so I asked him to get me the afghan from the living room. He darted out of bed—dashed to the bathroom —the kitchen—the basement—back to the bedroom—then asked breathlessly, accusingly, angrily, "What water? There are no broken pipes anywhere!" A normal misconception for the uninitiated. Mother, awakened by our hysterical laughter, learned the cause and joined in.

The drive to the hospital wasn't until noon, and then only because Sol was anxious. He dropped me off so he could park the car. I was put in a labor room with two other women and two empty beds. Once settled, I heard howls resounding and vibrating from the elevator shaft and markedly escalating when the doors opened. They came closer and jarringly entered my room, emanating from the mouth of a tall, rawboned woman. *"Tony!"* she shrieked. "TOOOHHH-NEEEE!" she yelled. She continued as though it were her mantra, changing abruptly to a normal tone of voice when answering the nurse's questions, then returning to the same volume and cadence as before. Sol entered the room in the middle of her performance and looked alarmed. Now all the beds were filled and our latest roommate's bellows overshadowed the moans, grunts and groans from the other two beds. We were all awaiting the arrival of this Atlas, this Herculean figure, who was being so loudly beckoned. And then he came, actually an emaciated-looking little runt of a guy—but that was in our eyes. Maybe he was an Adonis in hers.

My roommates left for the delivery room, one after another, including the new ones. It was a virtual procession, but I was still there. I didn't moan and groan or yell, took up too much energy, so when I told Sol to get the nurse because the baby was coming, he didn't believe me. Just then, Dad poked his head in the room and said, "Listen to her and do what she says. She knows." I had no idea he was there or how he got by everyone to be able to get to my room. Maybe he made delivery room friends when he substituted for Sol when Scott was born. No matter. Sol got the nurse, JoAnn arrived the evening of February 7, 1947, and the doctor came later, which didn't matter because all was well in spite of him. She had pretty blue eyes and

JoAnn, 9 months

blonde hair, enough to pull into a curl at the top of her head so everyone would know she was a girl. Sol spread the word throughout his world of what *he* had done—he was so very proud!

Mother nicknamed the baby "April Showers" because she cried loudly and long when she didn't get what she wanted. She didn't have to do that very often, however, because her big brother danced attendance on her all the time, and so, ultimately, did her younger sister. I never did learn her secret. We had some concerns about whether she would learn to speak because all she had to do was grunt and point and Scott got her what she wanted. And she was capable early on of getting what she wanted through out-and-out stubbornness. Like that stretch of no eating, when we worried and tried sweet talk, bribery, threats, to no avail.

"Eat, JoAnn."

"*No!*"

"You can't have dessert until you eat your dinner [or lunch, or breakfast]."

"*No!*"

A call to the doctor.

"JoAnn isn't eating. We're worried. What should we do"?

"She'll eat when she gets hungry," said wise Dr. Arnold. And again he was right.

When she got a little older, she did learn to talk (with more words than "no"), and her disposition became sunny. She loved being in front of a camera, hammed it up, liked to entertain and did it well. She also enjoyed mothering her younger sisters —and still does to this day.

Jo was the only one of our children to go to Israel. She and her fiancé Danny were sure it was a conspiracy to get her out of the clutches of this Southern gentile, but that wasn't the reason. She had just completed high school, did not want to go to college, had no plans or skills for the job market, and the opportunity to go overseas and to experience a far different way of life seemed ideal to get her out of

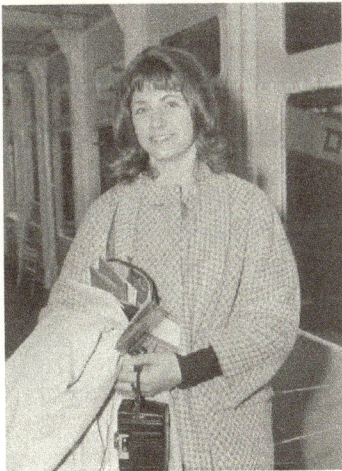

Jo, on her way to Israel.

her lethargy. She knew what she *didn't* want to do, but not what she *wanted* to do.

Brother Bob—who was visiting the States—offered to escort her, so she went, reluctantly. She experienced a different way of life, decided she did not like it, returned home, went to business school, married, and had a family of two wonderful boys, Keith and Brian. She and Danny also adopted a pretty three-year-old girl who had been so severely abused and neglected by her parents that they were in prison and their parental rights were terminated. Unfortunately, she was badly damaged, couldn't bond with anyone. When the treatment she received wasn't helping, they relinquished her so she could get a more intense treatment to help her as much as possible. Danny and JoAnn divorced due to irreconcilable differences in January 21,1983.

Then JoAnn moved to Denver, where she managed an apartment complex, was good at it. Unlike her mother, Jo can look at a house or apartment or any living quarters and see what can be done to improve its looks and functionality. She is also skilled at finding the furniture, decorations, paintings, and other things to make this happen at very reasonable prices. She worked skillfully at staging and enjoyed it. She started a business called

Distinctively Designed in which she used her talent. Her work is lovely, reasonably priced, and enjoyed especially by elderly people who have had to sell their homes and move into smaller quarters. She has also made pockets and other helpful things for wheelchairs and walkers, and she's sold furniture. Now, she has become a professional life coach, helping clients set and attain personal goals they want to achieve. She is a multi-talented, very enterprising woman.

Twenty-four years after her divorce from Danny, Jo married Dan, an orthopedic surgeon. My take on him was that he was a philandering, narcissistic, poor little rich kid who had been badly spoiled by his parents. He could sweet-talk, be solicitous, yet also be nasty and intimidating. Their marriage lasted for one very long year. It was a welcome relief when it was over.

Jo is the daughter who puts a GPS to shame with her wonderful sense of direction. She is organized, knows how to tell time, is never tardy, is action oriented, a doer.

Jo and her grandkids.

What she likes best of all is grandmothering. Her Grandchildren—Zander, Lucybelle, Caden, Dexter, and Ava—benefit from the marvelous job she does. She hugs and cuddles the little ones, and I marvel at the way she puts together projects that stimulate her grandchildren, increase their knowledge and their desire to search for more. She does it so successfully and she rejoices in it.

CHAPTER 19

THE INDEPENDENT THINKER

"It will stop as soon as she turns three months old," Dr. Arnold promised. "Until then, she will probably be eating every hour on the hour around the clock, so you need to get some help. You can't stay awake day and night and still take care of the other two children."

As usual, he was right. Toby, our beautiful, newborn infant had bronchial asthma and breathing was very difficult. I could handle bloody cuts and broken bones, but I froze when someone was choking. With the help of a night nurse, Toby did eat every hour on the hour around the clock. The asthma did stop right on time at the end of her first

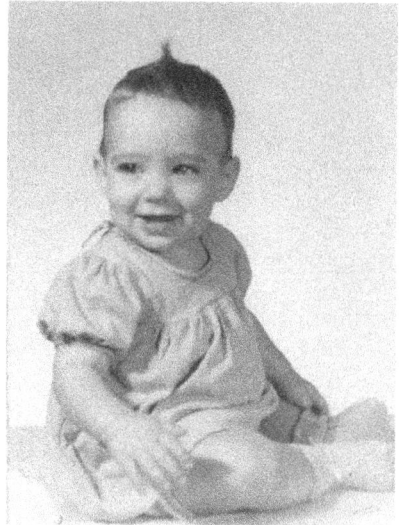

Toby, 9 months

three months. That was a blessing, and so was she, a veritable pleasure. She was a sweet, cuddly, warm, and lovable little girl—with a mind of her own.

It was apparent right from the start that she was an independent thinker, with an eye for the beautiful—and for the most expensive. When we shopped in the clothing department of any of the stores, she unerringly toddled up to the prettiest, priciest article there. She knew exactly what she wanted, never veered from her course, never tantrumed and never compromised. She preferred to do without rather than to settle for less than what she really desired, and she did so willingly, pleasantly, and without complaint. Her first spoken phrase, "Me do it myself," has continued to be her mantra throughout her life. Always with a smile, never an argument, she politely listens, then quietly goes about doing exactly what she wants exactly "her own way."

And her way most often is the best way for everyone—except for herself. (It's funny how she wasn't as serene about this behavior when her oldest son, Tavis, did the very same thing.)

She has always taken the time to smell the pretty flowers starting back in kindergarten. When her teacher called to ask if Toby's absence from school was due to illness, panic set in! She and her boyfriend Aaron had set off for school on time that morning as usual, and they certainly should have arrived there before the bell. When Aaron's mom and I scoured the neighborhood for the children, we learned they had leisurely strolled into the field, literally smelled the pretty flowers, and then wandered up the street to the corner convenience store. It was there we came upon them sitting on the floor, happily looking at the pictures in the comic books.

Not long after that, her friend Aaron and his older brother Mark, a second-grader and JoAnn's boyfriend, came to our house asking to speak to Sol. When he came into the room, they each went down on a knee and asked for the hands of our daughters in marriage. With a straight face Sol told them that was very nice of them but he thought they should wait a few years until they had jobs so they could take care of the girls. They bounced up to their feet, said "okay" and ran outside to play with the girls.

Years later, when she was very heavy with twins, Toby took the time to crouch on the sidewalk with her older son, Tavis, as they intently watched ants carry their heavy loads to their homes and potato bugs roll up into

balls. To my amazement and envy, when they were
through, she straightened into an erect position with
ease—and she didn't even use her hands to push herself
up!

Time has never been of consequence to Toby. It's
not that she can't read a clock or understand the concept,
it's just that it's low on her list of priorities. When drying a
dish she would lose herself in thought, and when she
finally returned from whatever planet she was visiting, the
dish had a high polish. At the bottom of her priority
barrel when she was in high school and college was
studying for exams and handing term papers in on time.
The schedules were ultimately met to the sacrifice of one
or more night's sleep, always a photo finish! In complete
contrast was her care of her children. When the twins
were born she didn't fall into the trap of waiting until the
last minute and rushing them through their routines. She
was not the "hose them down, fill them up, dump them in
bed" kind of mother. While she leisurely bathed the twins
with her older son looking on, she cooed to and played
with one baby while she talked to the other two in
soothing, unhurried tones. She thoroughly enjoyed each

of her children, and they responded in kind—and still do to the present time. What a strong determining factor motivation can be.

Toby's artistic talent, evident early on, was first brought to our attention—negatively—by her teachers,

Smokin', acrylic on canvas by Toby

not *draw* her name or any other words when she was learning cursive writing. Her penmanship looks beautiful even now but continues to be difficult to read. The teachers did, however, tell us that Toby had artistic talent and it should be encouraged. I was quite put out when they emphasized her talent because I was convinced that all of my children were talented and I didn't understand why they didn't understand that. They were right in their assessment of her skill, which took nothing away from the other children. The realistic representations in her paintings, most often of people, reveal not only their essence but seem to tell their stories. Her colors, subjects and composition are uplifting. She is highly critical of her work, as she has always been of herself. She was homecoming queen in her last year of high school. I never could understand why she can't see *pretty* when she looks in the mirror when she most certainly is.

Homecoming Queen

But her forte is mothering. When her sons were four and six, her ex-husband joined and became a zealot in a fundamentalist religion unknown and alarming to her. It was just after the Jonestown calamity, which made her nervous. After she graduated college, in her "do it herself" mode, she took action to leave Tucson with her children. She hated Tucson passionately, so without consultation or fanfare,

she went to San Francisco, found a job, returned home, packed up her belongings and the children, and set off for California. She had me appointed supervisor of the children a set number of times a week when they were visiting in Tucson, which was a bonus for me. San Francisco was unfamiliar to her—she knew no one there and she had no place to live. But she was undaunted. She was determined. She knew everything would be all right. I was exceedingly worried. She gave me her work address and phone number, tried to reassure me by telling me she would find a place to live, they'd be fine, and not to worry. I wasn't reassured, but she was right. She found a place, enrolled the children in school and day care, felt San Francisco was

not an ideal place to bring up children, and moved within a year to Sacramento, where she remains to this day.

Her sons, who are loving, independent adults with their own homes, visit her frequently. She feathered the nest so well that it was a virtual clubhouse for the boys and their friends, who still stop in to see Toby and who include her in many of their important events such as

Brandon, Toby, Cameron and Tavis at the twin's high school graduation.

engagement parties, weddings, and christenings. Being in her home with her family is basking in the sunshine no matter what the weather. A courageous, strong, determined woman, she has made an extraordinary success with what is most important in her life, her children!

Chapter 20

BONSAI

Time marched on and so did the babies, but this time the fetus was dead. I knew it was. I was convinced it was, but the doctor seemed unaware or unwilling to acknowledge it. I was not a novice at this pregnancy bit. This was my fourth time around, so, when movement stopped after having felt life at the beginning of the fourth month, I recognized something was very wrong. I said nothing at the start. I thought the perpetual activity with my children was so distracting I didn't notice the motion. I just didn't want to believe what I knew to be true. If I ignored it, maybe, magically, all would be well. By the fifth month, the doctor still said nothing and neither did I and everything remained the same. I was so upset by the sixth month I told Sol I was going to change doctors if my obstetrician didn't at least acknowledge that this pregnancy was going nowhere. He heartily agreed.

But my next appointment was different. X-rays were ordered, which confirmed my diagnosis, and my doctor explained that the fetus should have miscarried at the beginning of the fourth month, when it died. As we both knew it didn't and, he added, it might not until it reached term. He assured me I was in no danger if this should happen. He was wrong! No danger physically perhaps, but my mental health was going to be shot to hell if the fetus didn't abort right away. I couldn't conceive until I got rid of it, and I wanted six children. Also, carrying something dead inside of you did not make for pleasant dreams. The doctor said he could try to induce labor in the seventh month, an abortion, but he could not guarantee it would work.

So it began. Into the hospital, a drip in the arm and immediate contractions – hard ones – all day long. Nothing. The drip was removed at night so I could get uninterrupted sleep. Day two. A repeat of the procedure. Again, nothing. The morning of day five, the doctor said this would be it, the last chance. No abortion, no more drip. If no success, I would have to wait until the ninth month, when it would abort naturally. Five days of hard labor with no light at the end of the tunnel was a horrifying prospect!

Sol was wonderful. He came to the hospital in the morning before work and in the evening after checking on the children. He brought me news of the youngsters in delightful detail, news of his work and world affairs. We read, played cards and talked and talked. He was not only supportive but a positive thinker. He assured me that the fifth day would be the charm. It would be the day of victory and he was right—it was. The mission was accomplished.

I should have been relieved and happy. I was neither. I was exhausted and depressed. I was moved from the labor room to a semi-private room. We weren't released from the hospital quickly then, as is the practice today. I spent my time between crying and apologizing to my roommate. She had given birth to a preemie weighing just over two pounds and was rejoicing, as they had been trying to have a child for fifteen years. I was ashamed of carrying on in such a fashion when I knew I had three healthy children at home and would have more. That seemed to make no difference. I was mourning for the child I had looked forward to and lost. My roommate was kind and sympathetic.

Sol was tender and comforting. He gave me a plant, not a colorful blossoming one but a thoughtful one that was perfect for the occasion. It was a Bonsai tree with a card assuring happiness, a perfect gift of love, and it renewed me. After a few days, Sol took me home where the children waited. They had missed me.

CHAPTER 21

MY DIANE

I named her myself, not after a person, but after the theme song of an old silent movie: *Seventh Heaven*, with Charles Farrel and Janet Gaynor. It was a most appropriate name. I *was* in heaven when I saw her smile, my Diane. I wished she could smile all the while and not just for me, my Diane.

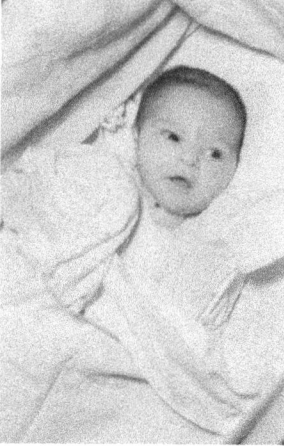
Diane, newborn

Diane was almost the entrée at our 1952 Seder dinner. My water broke as I was making matzo balls for thirty-two family guests expected by sundown. But she waited. She waited until the next day after we put her seven-year-old brother on the train for his first solo ride to Scranton. Then Diane made her grand entrance, our fourth child, our first brown-eyed baby, with a shock full of dark brown hair to match. She was beautiful. She most always was. We had some problems in the beginning, me with vertigo and Diane with laryngeal spasms that interfered with her breathing

142

and eating. A calcium supplement was an easy fix for her problems.

Diane was a serious little girl whose big eyes took in everything. She was quiet, and after an overnight with her girlfriend Liz Swados, Liz's father asked if she ever talked or if she simply didn't talk to him. There were times when Diane disappeared. We searched for her, only to find that she had taken herself to her bed for a nap. I had never experienced such a thing with any other children. Diane was unique, always, in many wonderful ways.

I think Diane invented active listening. For most of her life, she heard what was being said, was accepting, not judgmental, and always compassionate. She was a great storyteller, with real stories to tell. She acted them out with abandon to the delight of her audience, both young and old. Her special style of humor lightened spirits when things got tense. A favorite of hers was the airport story.

She had arrived with little time to spare to make her flight from her California pharmacy job to Tucson in time for her birthday party. She did her little dance—three steps to the left, three to the right—several times—then tapped the side of the security door four times on the right, four on the left—several times again. "Get in there, damn it!" she ordered herself. Time was of the essence. She rushed to the conveyor belt, dragging her luggage behind. Breathless, she flung her suitcases on the belt, then followed what she thought were the attendant's instructions. She swore the attendant had instructed *her* to get on the conveyor belt. "Another new rule," she thought, as she complied. She leapt onto the belt with aplomb, and regained her footing, when, to her horror, she saw the luggage x-ray inspection apparatus coming rapidly toward her. Quickly she stretched her arms out straight, crouched down, head to chest, and went through the screener without incident. Then, she gracefully swung her beautiful long legs around, dismounted with baggage in tow, and made her flight—just as the plane's doors were about to close. She regaled her birthday well-wishers with her story, laughing with each telling, to their enjoyment and hers. She had a happy birthday.

When we were all in the hospital, where her brother, Scott, had heart bypass surgery, she clowned around, told jokes, and cracked everyone up. It lightened our heavy tension and all was well at the end.

When she outgrew the young colt stage she became an exotic beauty. She was voted Pocahontas in junior high, which was similar to homecoming queen in high school. She was a model for a number of years, and it was disconcerting but fun to see her gazing at us in her bathing suit from big billboards situated in various spots in the city. She was physically active, very flexible, and worked for a time at a fitness spa. She had always enjoyed doing handstands, backbends, splits, cartwheels, and the like. I was never sure, when I was working in the kitchen,

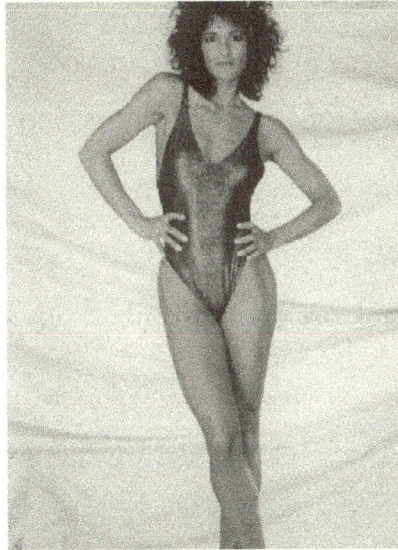

which part of her I was talking to, her head or her feet. Even in her forties and early fifties she could turn herself into a virtual pretzel.

Everything seemed wonderful until Diane turned fourteen years old, though I learned later on that it had started long before that time. That's when I noticed a dramatic change in her. The "in" thing was the "out" thing—out of classes, out of the house, defying authority in school and at home. Her peers set the tone and the rules, which usually broke the house rules. It was also the onset of the heavy drug scene in junior and senior high school, and I was worried. This was my fourth, not my first, adolescent—but no two children are alike, and this challenge was beyond all others.

Sol, Diane and I went for counseling, which was ineffective. I thought it was due to the intense resistance of Diane and Sol. It was years before I knew what the problems and causes really were. Emotional and verbal abuse were not recognized as issues at this time. Their ingredients were looked upon as discipline, toughening of the children, to be imposed as a right of parenthood. There was no awareness of the extent of damage it caused until the advent of Child Protective Services. In that and other ways, the helping professions didn't yet have words for much of what Diane was experiencing, so, in essence, through ignorance the figurative book was thrown at her.

An exceedingly painful episode occurred when the psychologist we were seeing told me I was an enabler, and I had to enforce, without exception, the consequences of broken rules. One of them was not to leave the house without our knowledge and consent. After a horrendous sleepless night of trying to find Diane, who had climbed out the window in the middle of the night, I sat her down and told her she would have to leave home and not come back. That was the clearly stated, well known consequence of her behavior. Crying, she asked where she should go. I told her it was her decision to make and that I was surprised she hadn't done so before she left. I asked her to let me know where she was. I also told her she needed to pack because she would have to leave in a couple of hours so I could get to work. Sobbing, she packed her things in cardboard boxes and large paper bags. She left, I went to work. She did not let me know her whereabouts, but she kept in touch with her sisters, who assured me she was safe. This was one of the few hardest things I've had to do in my life, and I think it did more damage to the two of us than any good.

The most horrendous impact was caused by her sick father on a power trip who abused, over-controlled, and denigrated all of the children, but chiefly Diane, the most vulnerable one. I was so busy with the family's survival, working and going to graduate school in Phoenix, that I was neither readily accessible nor aware enough to be protective. Tragically, the victim of the unhappy triumvirate of Sol, myself, and Diane . . . was Diane. She thrashed around in hurtfully unacceptable ways in her effort to extricate herself from the situation. She did it all—dropping out of school, drugs, teen pregnancies, marriage, divorce, and exotic dancing. Her overpowering father convinced her that she was a slut, stripped her of what self-esteem she had. It was not until she moved out of the house for a fair length of time that, in a telephone conversation with me a few days before her father and I were to leave for a trip to Italy, she told me she hated him and had a right to, because he had sexually molested her for years. She begged me not to divorce him, but I did.

And I have spent many hours and days castigating myself for not having recognized Sol's behavior. I worked for years helping children and families overcome, as best as they could, the effects of child sexual molestation and abuse. Why didn't I know? Why didn't the children feel comfortable enough to tell me? I still haven't been able to answer these questions to my satisfaction.

We ultimately learned that Diane had a chemical imbalance in the brain that resulted in bipolar and obsessive-compulsive disorders. Little was known about OCD back then, and not many people know much about it still. The repetitive behavior commonly related to the disorder seems strange, the tapping and counting, six steps this way then six steps that way, then six steps this way, again and again. Jack Nicholson portrayed it well in the movie *As Good As It Gets*. OCD manifests itself in many ways. An inability to keep appointments because compulsions make it impossible to be on time. An inability to curb the impulsive buying and returning of items, although you knew when you bought them they weren't needed but you were still compelled to get them. The impossibility of getting organized because what you are compelled to get you are also compelled to keep, can't throw anything out. The inability to manage money when you have the same amount of difficulty earning an income that you have controlling the outflow. The perpetual activity that goes on in the brain like loud static, saps energy, making you tired all the time. Counseling-type therapy helps marginally some of the time. Diane learned the techniques so well she could skillfully conduct the sessions herself. Drug therapy is often counterproductive. What helps one disorder exacerbates the other, and often the dosages given are so strong you sleep away days. No one had greater challenges than she—not even Job. The obstacles she had to face would have felled a lesser person, but not Diane.

When I was traveling back and forth from Tucson to Phoenix to graduate school, I conscripted friends and relatives to read some of my homework on tape so I could listen while I drove. Didn't want to waste that driving time. Without exception, Diane, the high school dropout, was the best reader of all, even better than my advanced-degree friends who didn't seem to know the meaning of punctuation. Diane's inflection, phrasing, and articulation made the written word come alive. She plied her skills occasionally at poetry readings and did an outstanding job. She was a prolific reader with excellent comprehension and an amazingly retentive memory.

She also wrote and illustrated, in her own special way. A half a cup of heart-wrenching guts, a half a cup of humor, a liberal sprinkling of compassion, mix well, and Diane's distinct individual style came out and grabbed you where you lived. She had boundless imagination and creativity, which she expressed when she did improvisations, or when she decorated her house

Celebrate, watercolor and ink, by Diane

and hung her favorite red spike-heeled shoes on the wall. She could take someone's discards, such as thrift-store items or things she found along the street, and with a twist or turn or the placement of them, turn them into lovely and interesting pieces of art.

She had great sales ability. With her enthusiasm, energy and charisma she could sell any product she believed in and she did her homework well. She worked at a variety of jobs, sold in novelty shops and boutiques, made floral arrangements, went on shoots as a photographer's assistant. Unfortunately she was unable, because of her severe case of OCD, to stay with any job for the long haul.

The doctors said she couldn't become pregnant. Then a miracle happened, daughter Taylor. She became the centerpiece of Diane's life, the most beautiful flower in her garden. Diane exposed her to the sunlight of all the possibilities of things she could become and nourished her with the sense that she could do and be whatever she made up her mind to

Diane with Taylor, her everything.

be. If there is something beyond redoubling efforts, Diane did it. She was determined to do the best possible for her little girl, and she did. She was a marvelous nurturer. She was an active participant in all of Taylor's endeavors—in school, in extracurricular activities, in social activities. She was forthright, took the time to make concrete and abstract concepts clear to Taylor—even defined OCD in terms she could understand when she was preschool age.

She managed to pass her humor on to her daughter. Watching them laugh together was good for the soul. Her humor and her daughter were her lifelines, and she needed them because of the many obstacles in her way, in even the simplest routine parts of her life.

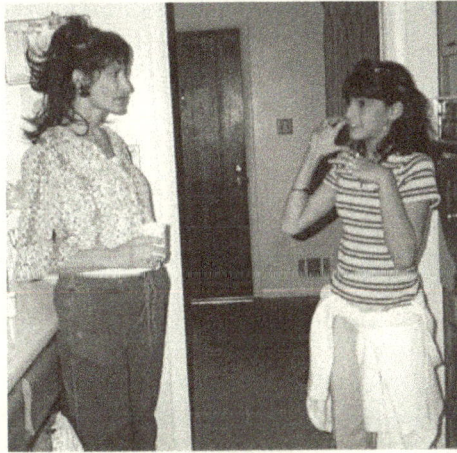

Like mother like daughter.

Diane taught her to accept people of all kinds and to respect their unique differences. She kept abreast of the activities available for children Taylor's age and encouraged her to take advantage of them. Diane instilled in Taylor a sound value system and the strength to stand up for herself and others whenever it is needed. Her hope for Taylor was that one or more of the possibilities she was exposed to would ignite a spark, a passionate interest that she would pursue and thoroughly enjoy throughout her life.

Diane was a strong participant in life. She looked, listened, and learned. She didn't let life fly by her. She tried to grab onto it and make use of it. Her indomitable will, incredible and lifesaving sense of humor, her compassionate concern for mankind and, primarily, her love for her daughter brought her through seemingly insurmountable problems. She contracted Hepatitis C when she was into drugs as a teenager, and it ultimately resulted in cirrhosis of the liver. She was a strong and amazingly courageous woman until her death at age fifty-six, and according to her sisters, beyond.

CHAPTER 22

SWEET SUE

Susan was enchanting from the start, pink cheeks with blue eyes and blonde hair, and the sweetest temperament. Of my six children, she was the first I watched enter the world, and she was beautiful. Her sunny disposition was challenged in the first three months of her life. Sister JoAnn had whooping cough, which Dr. Arnold said could be lethal for infants. He ordered that Susan not only be kept away from her sister, but from any of the rooms she had occupied. Confined to her second floor bedroom, Susan went "in and out the window" to the upstairs porch and nowhere else in the house until sufficient time passed. Her cheery nature never changed. It was a welcome relief to us all when we could be

Susan, 9 months

155

together at the same time in the same place. Petite as compared to her siblings, her sometimes-delicate appearance was misleading. She is strong, a powerful katrinka, and she takes care to remain so. She's an ardent exerciser, careful to the nth degree about her diet, believes in holistic, natural everything. That is her physical self. She has an incredible inner strength as well. She endured and overcame the damaging abuse by her father that she sustained as she was growing up. It took her singular determination and grit to not only surmount it but to direct the effects of it in a positive way through her writings and art.

She has always been unique and creative, from the Sweet Pea hippity-hop crawl of her infanthood to her unrivaled greeting cards of today. At an early age, she was a natural at sewing, fashioned costumes out of what was at hand for impromptu plays that she and her sisters performed.

Years later, she made her younger sister Debbie's lovely wedding dress. Her artistic talent was evident in her pottery. Her candle lamps, bowls, dishes, pitchers, etc., had her special touch that made them readily identifiable in the stores or shows. Customers specifically asked for her pieces and were proud to display and use them in their homes. She had outlets in Arizona, New Mexico, and California. Business was good, but her hands weren't. She tried everything—lotions, gloves—but nothing worked to heal her skin. She finally had to give it up and turned, instead, to painting. Even before she had any formalized art training, her work was outstanding. Her fine art hangs in the homes

Interrupted Sleep, **oil on masonite by Susan**

of people in different parts of the country who have purchased her pieces. She works in various media and has done portraits, commissioned work and—her preference—what comes out of her head or, as she puts it, her guts. Her work is eclectic, from real to surreal.

For years, Susan wrote short pieces, some philosophical, some humorous, and some plain quirky—at least by my lights. Subsequently, she began illustrating some of her writings, which evolved into a unique line of greeting cards called Pondering Pool—not the usual birthday, anniversary, thank-you, Hallmark variety. They are her own Susan-type sentiments

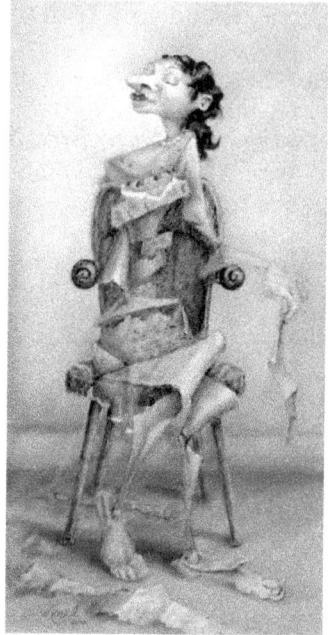

Perfect Pieces, **card image by Susan**

expressed through her skillful and remarkable creations, depictions of what goes on in her head and heart.

She married her wonderful husband Bill on September 18, 1976. He later left his graphic-arts job, and he and Susan became business partners in Pondering Pool. Bill handles the office work, fills the merchandise orders, and does the shipping, billing, etc. He and Susan jointly check out the printing of the cards and more. It is definitely a partnership, and a good one. Bill is supportive, protective, has a great sense of humor, and plays a mean guitar. He's a keeper.

Since Susan's cards have been on the market, she has received a steady flow of letters, calls, and emails from people around the country who have been deeply touched by them. They not only thank her and encourage her to keep the cards coming, but they ask about her, from where and how she gets her ideas. They want to meet her, feel a kinship with her, which is rewarding and replenishing to her.

The great majority of her work is predicated on Diane, her trials and hardships, the agony and laughter caused by her OCD and bipolar afflictions. Susan was exceedingly close to Diane—drew with her, wrote with her, suffered with her, cried with her, and laughed with her in spite of the darkness. She has a deep understanding of Diane's demons, which she reflects so movingly in her writings that they are being used by many psychiatrists and psychologists.

She presently makes posters of her cards, has published a book, makes unusual dolls out of clay, photographs and makes cards from them, and is working on having her characters animated. Her work is ever evolving. Planful, persevering, talented, and determined, she can and does anything she makes up her mind to do, and she does it well. It is always exciting to see where she will be going next. Sweet Sue, she's an amazing gal.

CHAPTER 23

DEBBIE WHO DID IT RIGHT

From the beginning, she did everything right. It was May 14, 1956—a year and a half after Susan entered our family—that she joined us. Expecting our sixth and last child, we were adding a bedroom and playroom to our house in anticipation. We hoped the rooms would be finished in time for the baby's arrival. They

Debbie, 6 months

were—just a gasp before our beautiful brown-haired, brown-eyed Deborah Ellen, aka Debbie (her preference), came into our lives. I'm sure she planned it that way.

Debbie dedicated herself to doing everything right—apologize for everything even though she wasn't involved—cause no problems, make no waves. She succeeded—if you don't count the time she ate almost a whole bottle of baby aspirin when she was six and had to have her stomach pumped. Or the day she walked in front of her little girlfriend's swing and was hit on the forehead, resulting in six or eight stitches. These incidents took place when she was of pre- and primary school age. In college, it was the totaling of Toby's car, a trauma that, fortunately, left no lasting ill effects. Since these were accidents, not planned occurrences, they don't really count.

Debbie—our sweet, serious, curly-headed little girl—was timid and tense, tried desperately to avoid her dad's wrath. Being the youngest, she heard and saw the flack her older siblings were experiencing from him and feared it. Doing everything that was expected, she succeeded in keeping the waters around her free of even a ripple. She attended college for a short time after high school but, having no particular direction, decided not to waste money, so she quit and went to work. Like the other children, she left home at her earliest opportunity.

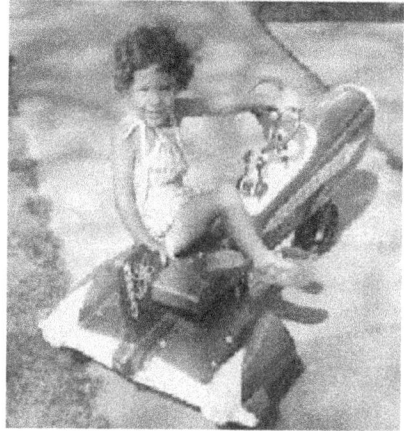

Debbie always loved movies and was particularly enthused about media classes. Her teacher's encouragement set the course toward her future career. From virtually her first job behind the scenes on TV in Tucson, she set out on her media road, loved it and excelled at it—still does. She is my upwardly mobile, female executive daughter.

Debbie and Barry married in 1979. A nice down-home boy of many talents, he wasn't open to exploring new horizons. Debbie was open to the world. During this time she had a frightening bout with melanoma. She faced it, did what had to be done, took necessary precautions and charged on with her life without complaint. When in 1991, the marriage became too confining, she and Barry had an amicable divorce.

Snorkeling in protective gear.

Debbie took a job in cable TV in Denver. She moved from one station to another, beginning her climb up the corporate ladder. Dedication to her work did not interfere with her romance with Bill, whom she met shortly after settling in Denver. His many

Bill and Debbie toasting at their wedding reception.

and varied talents and skills opened the door to new adventures and interests for Debbie. Never one for the great outdoors, she now goes snorkeling, sailing, fishing, hiking and more. (Mindful of skin cancer, her attire for the great outdoors is amazingly awesome— not the usual fashion plate on planet earth, but from somewhere else in outer space!)

Debbie is a prolific reader, a voracious viewer of movies (which is a necessity for her job—how clever of her), a gracious hostess (she loves to entertain), and an accomplished cook.

Irma and Debbie at Debbie's first seder.

She takes pleasure in traveling to new places though she may not be able to point them out on the map, geography not being her forte. She is directionally challenged, like her mother, and maternal grandfather—can't help it, it's in the genes! She thoroughly enjoys her trips to Europe, the Amazon, etc., meeting new people, experiencing new cultures.

Debbie packs her life full, makes the most of each day, and still finds the time to laugh and cry, listen to and advise, lend a hand and a heart, to family and friends. From a timid little girl full of worry and fear, she has blossomed into a confident, self-directed, successful executive; a loving wife, daughter, and sister; and an all around-marvelous person to have the privilege to be with and to know. I'm so very proud of her.

PART FOUR

GOINGS ON

CHAPTER 24

THE BRAILLE EXPERIENCE

There was that brain-numbing time when I had to escape or the cerebrum would atrophy. The time when the older kids were at school, the young ones were bedded down for naps, the housework was done, the laundry was churning, awful soap operas were on TV, my book was finished. I couldn't get out, I was stuck. I loved my children, but it took more than kid talk to keep the gray cells working. I had to find something to do, and I did.

The Sisterhood of my Temple was giving Braille lessons at a time that didn't interfere with my domestic or maternal chores. After a year of classes and practice, I received my Braille certification from the Library of Congress, which was more exciting than getting either my BA or my MSW. I thought mastering this foreign (to me) language was a wondrous accomplishment, but I didn't expect the news media to feel the same way.

They did an article including photographs of my family and me, but I don't know why. I certainly wasn't the first or only person who became certified. It was exciting nonetheless. And it became a lengthy process because of our number-six child, Debbie, who wasn't yet two years old. She had to stand on an ottoman to be seen in the picture. Unerringly, she got down from her perch at the precise moment the shutter was clicked, time after time after time. The photographer was patient and amused, seemed

Eggertsville Mother of 6 Cited for Skill With Braille

1957

Vaults Domestic Hurdles, Transcribes for Blind

SOL FISHER AND SCOTT, 13, ADMIRE LIBRARY OF CONGRESS CERTIFICATE
On the Steps: Deborah, 2; Susan, 3½; Diane, 8; Toby, 9; JoAnn, 11

not to mind the number of shots wasted. It was great fun for us all.

We moved to Tucson in 1957 before I had a chance to repay the Sisterhood for the Braille lessons by transcribing for them.

They say if you don't use a foreign language, you'll lose it, and this was true of Braille as well. Shortly after unpacking and settling into our new home and knowing that Sisterhoods of Reformed Temples throughout the country sponsored works for the blind, I asked to join the Braille program at our new Temple in Tucson.

"Braille?" they asked.

"Yes, Braille." I answered.

"Do you know it?" they asked.

"I just learned it." I said.

"Will you teach it?" they asked.

"I'll try," said I. And that's how it all began.

It was a challenging, rewarding experience, which

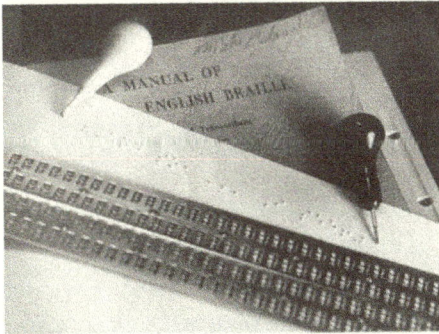

Braille stylus

began with a class of about 10 students and mushroomed into an organization of almost 150, all working volunteers. The clever, creative name we gave it was Books for the Blind. We taught classes in Braille to sighted people who then transcribed books into Braille for the State School for the Deaf and Blind, college students, and people in business. We made many copies from an original on our donated duplicating machine, and we bound our own books. We had volunteers read books on tape, and those who could typed large-print books on our donated large-print typewriter, all for students.

It was a revelation, a marvelous learning experience—not just the Braille, but the contact with blind people for whom we made books. A rabbi who'd taught my religious school class when I was in high school was the only blind person I had been in contact with up close and personal. I knew he was knowledgeable, that he could get around with the help of his cane, and that he had a reader. And that was all I knew. From my experiences with Books for the Blind, I learned there is far more that a blind person can do than what he can't.

Barbara was one of the first recipients of our work. She was a young, attractive woman who played piano beautifully. She taught it for a while to some of my children. She could read Braille right through her lovely white gloves. Amazing! It wasn't long before she married Bob, and they raised a family of three children at last count. Bob, also blind, operated a stand with coffee, snacks and sandwiches at a downtown business complex.

I was fascinated with some of the comments I heard at conferences. I particularly recall the response to a picture of the galaxy displayed in an exhibit. An enterprising person had, with the use of wire and different-size beads, fashioned this picture so that the relative dimensions and distances among the planets could be simulated. It was a big success, unlike the attempt to create a Dr. Seuss picture with the use of feathers, beads, sequins, fabrics, and other kinds of materials. I also remember one blind woman laughing at herself as she related that she thought all chickens had four legs until she held one at a farm. She had been excited. She'd thought the hen was unique with its two legs. She had never before encountered a living chicken, and her family always had four drumsticks at their dinner table. Small wonder when the word was out that she was delightedly surprised.

Our organization was interdenominational. Volunteers came from throughout the community, all dedicated and vigorously involved. Many of us were activists, attempting to bring about changes that ultimately did come to pass. The State School for the Deaf and

Blind was a marvelous facility with all of the state-of-the-art equipment and the easiest students, at least the blind students, to teach. This was in the days before blind children were mainstreamed into the public school system.

We learned how isolated the children felt in their own neighborhoods when they were home during holidays and for the summer. They had no opportunity to mingle with the sighted neighbor children and vice versa. The neighbor children shunned or made fun of them because they had no opportunity to get to know them. Then our goal expanded. It was not only to make books for the children but to try to change the laws so those who wanted to could attend school in their own neighborhoods. We also learned that the State School would not accept children who had multiple handicaps. Their parents supported our efforts. They hoped that space and money would then be directed to developing programs to meet their children's special needs.

The superintendent of the school, who had been there since the Stone Age, was adamantly opposed. He felt it would result in a mass exodus from the State

School. They would have to close their doors. This, of course, was ludicrous. Having been in his position so long, he had a lot of clout with the State Legislature, and his opposition was the biggest block to the proposed desegregation. A group of us were allowed or invited, I can't remember which, to present our case at a Senate hearing on the subject. Two young college students, for whom we made books, came from a unique situation. Their mother was blind from birth, as were two of her four children. She knew what the children were capable of doing and saw to it there was no malingering. Both children were independent, self-sufficient, and bright. One of them joined us at the hearing. As we were driving to Phoenix, she cautioned us. She said she was going to stumble and bumble around in the hearing room and act humble and everlastingly grateful because, as she put it, that's what was expected of blind people. She was willing to enlist their pity if that's what it took to get the bill passed. This was abhorrent to us, but we went along with it. Although she was quite an actress, the bill did not pass at that session. It did pass subsequently, and the State School is still in operation to this day.

My most clever act in this entire endeavor was to name Betty as my successor when, in 1964, I had to relinquish my position as head of the organization in order to become gainfully employed. She'd been one of my first Braille students, and she served with dedication and efficiency for many years until the program was disbanded. The State School for the Deaf and Blind paid tribute to her and Books for the Blind at their graduation exercise the year we went out of business. Which proves the old adage: "If you live long enough . . ."

CHAPTER 25

SOL: PART II

When Sol was mustered out of the army, I discouraged him from resuming his pre–World War II job in the pants factory with his patronizing and ill-paying cousin. He accepted a job selling curtains wholesale throughout New York state. It was offered by an affluent, honest, and generous friend of my parents. Sales was a new experience for him, and he was nervous. Armed with son and toidy seat, I accompanied him at his request and literally pushed him out of the car and into the stores until he discovered he had a natural flair for selling. Within a short time, he hired his friend Dick to cover the state of Pennsylvania. Business was good.

When the bottom fell out of the curtain business, Sol and Dick explored opening a men's haberdashery on the University of Syracuse campus. I accompanied them to search for a house for us. I had the "toidy seat" and son in one hand, and a diaper bag filled with bottles and our infant girl in the other. We put a deposit on a beauty of a house with bay windows and window seats. It was exciting. We returned home to consult with my conservative attorney father regarding the entire venture before making a final decision. Our business knowledge and experience was minimal, our financial resources virtually nonexistent, and the risks were high. The whole undertaking was subsequently abandoned.

After a period of inertia, Sol took a job as salesman in a "direct to you" upholstered furniture factory, making forty dollars a week to start. This while still supporting his mother, sister, wife, and two children. He knew he'd have to move up fast. His "hard sell" approach was very successful with the customers, though it made me cringe. He was a crackerjack salesman no matter what the product. His salary increases were not commensurate with the spiraling sales he generated. His employer was patronizing, giving him compliments and gifts—of used, torn but washed, *starched and ironed* handkerchiefs and socks—instead of additional money.

As he had done with his cousin, Sol accepted this without argument or rancor. I resented it and groused about it. The carrot his boss held out to him was that he had Sol in his will—meaning that Sol would get the business when he died. The boss's father was pushing ninety! We learned much later that his boss followed in his father's footsteps. Sol quit his job, and we blazed a new trail to the land of opportunity in Arizona. He bought a janitorial business in which he had no prior experience, but he made a go of it. He added a flue-cleaning business, which also did well. As a "do it myself" kind of guy, it was hard for him to rely on others to do the hands-on work. He always worked hard, two and three jobs at a time when necessary. He pleased his bosses, who always wanted to keep him, and he was confident in the results of his labor.

When he became ill and had to sell his business, he went to work for the city in the HUD program. He enjoyed working in an office where his skill with numbers held him in good stead until he was no longer able to compute due to his disability. It was then he took a disability retirement.

Sol was able to envision things. I couldn't. This was handy when it came to our living quarters. When we searched for a larger home in Buffalo to accommodate our expected fourth child, I couldn't foresee how the one we were considering could be viable. It was a four-bedroom, two-bath house in the suburbs. I didn't like the decor. It had a silhouette of a nude woman on the recreation room floor in the basement, dirty diapers on every step of the carpeted stairway from the living room to the second floor, very large and some small decals of cavorting nude women covering the walls of the breakfast room and a mural of a hunting scene on the kitchen wall. All I could see was the filth and smell the stench of the moment. Sol could anticipate the positive effects that soap, water, disinfectant, and minimal cosmetic changes could engender.

Sol was good at remodeling, wasn't even hesitant to knock down walls to enlarge rooms. Thank goodness for that! We enjoyed this home for many years. The first change he made in our last home together was to knock out the wall from the bathroom off the master bedroom and put in a door to the hall. By this time, there were eight of us, and easy access to both bathrooms was essential.

Sol had boundless energy, which he used productively at work, at home, and at play. He was competitive and a good bridge player, not so serious that he couldn't kibitz and still score high. His bowling was far superior to mine, which allowed us to stay in the upper echelon in our couple's league. He prided himself on his strength and superb physique, and he excelled in sports and any physical endeavor he undertook. That's what made the draining away of these attributes doubly hard for him and made him doubly hard for everyone he encountered.

CHAPTER 26

DAD, OUR FIRST ADOLESCENT

Three years after Mother's death, Bob, Sol, and I watched Dad pace up and down, back and forth, in anguish in our living room.

"There's a woman in California," he said. "I've known her for years through work. She's bright, attractive, a nice person, but she is almost twenty years younger than I. Mother met her and liked her." Pause. "I've been lonely since Mother died, and I've thought of marrying again, but . . . "

Dad

"But what, Dad?" we chorused. If there was ever a man we knew who shouldn't, almost couldn't, live alone, it was Dad. He'd been a lost soul since Mother's death.

"What's the problem? Have you asked her? What did she say?"

"We've talked about it and she wants to get married but . . . "

"But what, Dad?"

Our voices raised the second time around.

What will people think?"

"What people?" we asked. "What difference does it make what people think? It's how *you* feel and what *you* think that's important. Would you like to have her as your wife?"

"Yes. She's intelligent, understands the business world, and she's interested in many things and is interesting."

"So?" we asked.

"Well, you know Mother was very sick for the last several years of her life, and it's been three years since she died, and I'm a lot older than this woman, and . . . "

"And what?" we asked. Then the light dawned.

"Are you worried that you can't perform sexually?" his son Bob forthrightly asked in this sudden reversal of roles.

"Yes!" Dad answered, relieved that it was out in the open for discussion. "She said we should go away together for a week or a weekend and if it turns out it isn't a problem we can get married."

"Great idea!" we asserted.

"But she's talking about sleeping together *before* we get married!" he exclaimed. A more straight-laced guy never lived. Here he was, in his sixties, so she was in her forties. They were both certainly of age and consenting adults, or they would be if he consented.

"Go for it!" said the cheering section.

"I'll think about it," said Dad. "Do you really think it would be alright?" our boy asked timidly.

"Absolutely," we responded.

We don't know whether they took that little side trip, but they became engaged and then the issue revolved about where the wedding should take place.

Fredericka wanted it in her hometown in California with her family and friends. Dad was adamant it should be in his hometown with his family and friends. So it was held in the rabbi's study in Buffalo where his family—and most particularly, mother's sister Aunt Mabel—was in attendance. I don't know if the latter was of such importance because it made him feel he had the tacit

Aunt Mabel

approval of Mother, or if it was of importance because Aunt Mabel was so instrumental in selecting him as her brother-in-law those many years ago. She was wonderfully supportive.

"Barney," said Aunt Mabel, using Dad's nickname, "was a wonderful husband to my sister. No one could have given her more in love and in material things. There is nothing further he can do for her and he is entitled to go on with his life. I'm happy he won't be alone." She

Dad and Fredricka honeymooning aboard S.S. Independence, June, 1959.

stated this emphatically to the skeptics—and there were some—but her approval won them over.

Fredericka and Dad went on an extended honeymoon cruise. Upon their return, we gave them a welcoming, tasty, noisy reception with family, friends, and the children in attendance. As much as I intellectually approved of Dad's second marriage, I did have uncomfortable feelings about her "taking Mother's place," foolish as I felt this was at my age. This notion dissipated when I overheard an exchange between them one day at their home. Dad was leaving for a golf game and Fredericka asked when he anticipated returning so she could have lunch ready for him. His "I'll be back when I get back" response was a shocker to me. Never had he ever spoken in such a fashion to Mother. I realized Fredericka married a man far different from the one who married my mother. Dad had danced attendance on Mother throughout their married life, even before from what I heard. Fredericka danced attendance on Dad. They lived a good life, traveled and entertained a lot and enjoyed one another's company. It was wonderful for him, for us, and for Fredericka as well. After almost twenty years of marriage, Fredericka suffered a long and painful bout with cancer. Dad nursed her until her death in 1975.

CHAPTER 27

WHAT?!

"You did *what?*"

I knew it! It was bound to happen. I was wrong. I thought a fundamental tenet of our country was freedom of religion, to worship in the belief of your choice or not at all if that should be your desire. This *is* a Christian country, just like a lot of people said. I knew it wasn't anti-Semitism, although that was and is still living and well. It was proselytizing and I hated it! That's what I got for living in an all Catholic neighborhood.

But I grew up in the same kind of neighborhood and, except for a few bouts with anti-Semitism, like Bud Christiansen calling me a dirty Jew when we were in grade school, nothing untoward happened to me. It did feel really good, though, when I flattened him with a lucky punch before I ran home to ask my mother what being a "dirty Jew" meant. Except for that glitch, it was wonderful living there.

But they didn't have those comic books when I was young. The ones with Jesus on the cross and blood in living color dripping down the pages. Those comic books certainly got the children's attention. And all the talk about sins and baptism and confession probably scared and confused them. And now my first-grader came home from school full of excitement, and she said . . .

"What did you say, JoAnn?"

"I crossed myself three times today."

"You did what?"

"I crossed myself three times today."

"What?"

"I crossed the street by myself three times today."

To say I felt a fool would be a gross understatement. I did commend myself for taking the time to clarify the situation. Kind of like counting to ten before exploding. And so, to fracture a phrase, all was well because it ended.

CHAPTER 28

THE SOUTHWEST GHOST

Tampa, St. Petersburg, Miami, Phoenix, and Tucson were cities of opportunity in the '50s. We needed new opportunities. Sol's boss was in continuing good health, so we decided not to wait for him to die. Our children were growing and so was the demand for a greater income. Florida was sunshiny, interesting, hot and humid—very humid—which is why their foliage is so lush and why we turned to the West, to Tucson. Sol scouted the area, then called, full of enthusiasm. He found a business and house combination for sale. Would I be willing to pull up roots and move to the wide-open spaces far away, to a two-bedroom home with an office? Of course! Home is wherever our family is, and since they'll be with us, wherever we are will be home.

The next weeks were a flurry of activity. We tossed useless stuff from the attic to a truck below to be taken to the dump. We arranged with a realtor to sell our house. We sold furniture and other items by candlelight (there was a power outage), and packed. At last the time had come, October of '58. We loaded the six children, our black cocker spaniel Queenie, and our most essential belongings into our wagon, revved up the motor, and were on our way. Many of our neighbors turned out trailing behind us while they waved goodbye as we drove down the street. It was very touching.

The trip was a long one, but far more comfortable than those of our pioneer ancestors. We had air conditioning, cushioned seats, shock absorbers, and hotels for dinner and a good night's sleep, all along the way. Queenie was the first out of the car when we stopped, and into the car when we boarded again, as the scratches on the door attested. Sol did all the driving and I did all the children-tending and entertaining. It was an adventure, exciting and fun for us all.

Five days on the road and we were finally there, in Tucson, driving to our new home. We saw mesquite, cactus, and palm trees rather than the maple and elm of Buffalo, many swimming pools, and a lot of sun. There were very few sidewalks, a mix of residential and business areas due to peculiar zoning or maybe no zoning. Patio walls encased the rear of most of the houses, either imprisoning the residents onto their property or preventing outside people from entering. In either case, it didn't look very friendly.

Got to our house before the moving van, which gave us a little time to case the joint. The front door led us directly into the living room, which was wide, but with little depth. Beyond it was a bedroom/office combination, inadequate for either. A hallway to the left of the living room joined the two real bedrooms with the one bathroom halfway between them. A dining area was to the right of the living room, with the kitchen behind it. The front and backyards had only sand, like being at the beach but without ocean or lake.

There was a small, uncovered patio in the rear and a minute front porch. We needed a shoehorn to fit our family of eight plus a dog into this cracker box, but we knew it was temporary. Seeing it made it even more temporary than we had expected.

When the van arrived, the beds went up quickly in the *real* bedrooms—for the girls, two bunk beds in one and twins in the other. A flimsy gerrymandered wall divided the office into an office/bedroom and a bedroom, both imperfect. Sol and I were crammed into the bedroom on one side and Scott in the office/bedroom on the other.

In our naiveté, we sold all of our upholstered furniture thinking it would be too hot and inappropriate for the desert. The rattan furniture, which had been the den furniture in Buffalo, became our living room set. The piano, coffee table and end tables just fit. The dining room set left the narrowest of paths for walking and shifting chairs in and out. Everything else remained on the diminutive piece of concrete outside in the back— uncovered in barrels, crates, and wardrobes subject to the elements. "No problem," we were told "It's always dry in the desert." Awakening the next morning, I looked out the uncovered window, nudged Sol and asked, what that white stuff was that was falling down from the sky. "First time in fifty years!" they said. A likely story, I thought.

There was much to do. Had to learn the janitorial business: meet the crew, learn the accounts, the city, and the day-by-day operation, to say nothing of Spanish, Mexican style. Had to uncrate and put everything away, but not until after an exterminating company rid us of the uninvited roaches that homesteaded the kitchen. Had to learn where the schools were to enroll the children. Had to adjust to the many differences between life in the big Eastern city and that in the small Western town. Tucson was not heavily populated. The main streets that were paved were wide and traffic was light. What a pleasure! The pace in this town was slow, partly due to the heat, and living was relatively easy and casual. Blue jeans and T-shirts were the accepted dress code for boys in high school as opposed to the slacks, white shirt, and tie back East. However, the high school dean of women laid down an edict that girls couldn't wear black patent leather shoes with skirts because it would reflect their panties. We were not sure what her hang-up was but were very sure she had one. The girls went Western right away. Scott was more sophisticated, so he did it his way, learning and going spelunking (caving).

We had a panic attack in the midst of the uncrating. We lost four-year-old Susan! We went up and down the unfamiliar streets, for what felt like a millennium, calling her name. At long last, she walked toward us holding the hand of a large man, Mr. Hoover. She had wandered off to explore the neighborhood, lost her bearings, didn't know the address, and was crying her heart out when this nice man befriended her. He was a long-distance trucker, a father of nine children who had just come off the road, so he was unaware there were new neighbors. He had the patience of a saint. He had calmed her, and played a game of "Is this the house? Does this one look like it? Don't worry, we'll find it." What a great guy, and how relieved we were. And so we settled into our home on the vast Western frontier.

We had moved to Tucson toward the end of October '57, and suddenly it was December and Chanukah was almost upon us.

Although we were still learning the front door from the back of our new life, we found a teenage neighbor down the street, willing and able to baby-sit. We didn't know a whole lot about her, but she was the second of eight children in a "his, hers and theirs" type family, so we figured she had some on the job training. She was a year or two older than fourteen-year-old Scott.

After an early dinner, Scott, Sol, and I took off on our brief gift-shopping mission. We didn't want to leave the girls with a new sitter in an unfamiliar house for long, so we rushed through our shopping and hurried back. Then came the trauma! There were police cars in front of *our* house with their lights flashing? What did that mean? Why were all of those people clumped around the front of our house? Who were they? Neighbors? Where were the kids? What happened?

The police were so busy scouring the area around our house, they couldn't take time to talk to us. The neighbors were as puzzled as we were. A stranger came toward us.

"I'm Mr. Castle," he said. "Your children are at my house and they are fine. Come with me. You can see for yourself."

He lived directly across the street. There they were, our five daughters, lined up on the couch, tense, hands clasped in their laps, with our babysitter hunkered down nervously in a nearby chair. They looked frightened but well, and then they told their story. It was incredible but they all swore by it.

The four of them, babysitter and three sisters, were in the living room talking. They heard footsteps outside and became anxious. The sitter, as protector, armed herself with a butcher knife from the kitchen, just in case. (That was pretty scary to us, as we listened.) The little ones were asleep. The girls moved from the living room to the bedroom wing of the house. Suddenly, the piano began to play! A tune! Who was playing it? They were alone in the house. Someone must have broken in, an intruder! They couldn't get to the front or back doors without going through the living room, and that's where the piano was. None of them were going in there. All they could do was yell! And that's what they did, via the high open window. They screamed so loud they woke the babies, who ran through the hall, fast as lightening, crying—right past the feared living room! Of course, they didn't know what to be scared of. Then all the girls yelled and screamed in chorus. They made such a racket that Mr. Castle heard them across the street and came to their rescue.

In a panic they told him what happened. He scouted the area, tried to assure them nobody was there now and urged them to come outside so he could take them to the safe haven of his house. They were too terrified. They absolutely would not go to the living room to get to the door. He finally took the screen from the bedroom window and out they climbed, all six of them, one at a time. The police were called and responded quickly. They searched on top of and all around the house for signs of an intruder—nothing! The children were safe in the Castle's home, where they had cotton candy from their machine and, like a spoonful of sugar, it helped the youngsters calm down. Then they waited and we finally came.

After bestowing our heartfelt thanks on our new neighbors, we returned home. When we unlocked the door Scott went directly to the upright piano to inspect it. As soon as he lifted the lid, out flew a huge, fat moth!

Our interpretation of the event was that the moth hit against the strings in his Herculean effort to escape from his prison. The girls' insist that someone broke in and played a tune on the piano. They cannot explain how this person could enter and leave the house without a trace or why anyone would break in simply to play the piano. Nothing was taken and nothing was disturbed— except the children, who certainly were. The question that remains is who came out—the ghost or the moth? Sol, Scott, and I are convinced it was the moth, and the girls are adamant that it was the ghost. They were unyielding on the subject then and, over four decades later, they continue to be.

CHAPTER 29

SOUTH OF THE BORDER

Pitch dark, middle of the night, and the phone was ringing. Who the devil could it be?

Sol answered, sounded incredulous, said: "Be there as soon as I can."

"What's wrong? Who was that? Be where?"

"The Nogales, Mexico, police department. You won't believe this. Our man, Jim, took our truck across the border. He got drunk, was picked up and put in jail. He asked the police to call me because our truck's been impounded!" Sol rolled out of bed. "I've got to get the truck back right away so we can use it tomorrow."

"I'm going with you," I stated emphatically. "I wouldn't miss it for the world. Just think, our first trip to Mexico, and in the middle of the night—sounds like a spy movie."

We dressed quickly, told Scott where we were going and that we'd be back as soon as possible. There was no traffic on the freeway and it was too dark to enjoy the scenery. We made the sixty miles in less than an hour and spent almost a half-hour trying to find the police station. Its narrow entry was jammed between two stores. On the other side of the door was a cramped, steep stairway, eerie in the dimly lit hallway. At the top was a tiny office on one side and a few cells on the other. It seemed this was not just the police station but also the jail. The lone policeman on duty who met us spoke *pock inglés*, and that with such a heavy accent we could barely understand anything he said. We spoke no Spanish. Our talk with one another was stilted and sparse. Any communication we accomplished was through gestures and body language.

He finally took us to Jim's cell. It was stark, grim and dark, far more frightening than inviting. Jim was disheveled, embarrassed, and chagrined. He mumbled apologies, couldn't look us in the eyes. He recounted his short jaunt to visit with a female friend, which didn't work out. He stopped for a few drinks to drown his sorrow. He remembered very little of what had happened after that. He somehow got into a scuffle with someone, over who-knew-what, and that's why the police were called. The way he looked, it had to have been a major fight. He was not being held in jail overnight only to sleep it off. He never made clear why he was being held for several days, but that's how long it took before his release. We could do nothing for him, so we left to negotiate the release of our truck.

Our language problem was frustrating to the point of ridiculousness. My knowledge of Spanish was so abysmal that, when a customer clearly enunciated an order to me, I spelled it my way – the wrong way. I didn't know that "j" was pronounced like "h" and two "ll"'s in the middle of a word was pronounced like "y." It was small wonder the men had a difficult time locating the job sites I wrote down for them until I finally had the good sense to ask everyone to spell names for me. Therefore, it was nothing short of miraculous that the policeman was able to have us sign the appropriate forms in the appropriate places and to direct us to where our truck was impounded.

Dawn was beginning to brighten the sky, and we had to hurry home before the children needed to eat and leave for school. I drove the car and Sol the truck and it was light enough to see the many shadings of green on the low rolling hills and the red and gray of the strip mines and the desert growth. Although this was our first trip to Mexico, we could not describe Nogales to the children despite the hours we spent there. Jim returned to work after a few days, still sheepish. He remained with us for a number of years, with never a repeat of his misadventure.

We returned to Mexico many times. At first it was to sightsee and shop in the narrow stores that lined the two-block strip. The shopkeepers aggressively hawked their wares. They walked in front of, beside, or behind us, telling of the bargains and showing samples of their merchandise. There was pottery, Mexican tile, Folklorica skirts and dresses, patio dresses, liquor, chess sets, bull whips, powder kegs, jewelry, leather goods, purses of all kinds and colors, shawls, hats, jackets, perfumes, a multitude of goods—and sameness from shop to shop. The bargains were everywhere. A price was given and we were expected to haggle. I disliked that and was very poor at it. I preferred to shop in the stores where the price was fixed.

My nephew Roni was skilled at it. It is the accepted method of transaction between Arabs and Jews in Israel, his homeland. He bartered exceedingly well. When he visited us at age thirteen, he wanted to bring presents home to his family. He bought a leather purse for his mother and wanted a chess set for his father, and a bull whip, powder keg, snorkel, and steer horns for himself. He saw a perfect chess game for his father in one of the shops. In an offhand manner, he asked the price of the item. When he was told the cost, he turned up his nose, said the price was too high, it wasn't worth it and began to saunter out of the shop. The storekeeper followed him and asked for a counter offer. They haggled back and forth with no results. The shopkeeper, looking at this cocky young kid, figured he didn't know anything about chess so he set up the board and challenged him to a game. Roni accepted the challenge without enthusiasm, put on the most bored air and wandered off between turns to check out the other items he wanted for himself. In spite of his roaming, he won the game in short order with aplomb. The shop owner was so amused and taken by him that Roni got all the items he wanted at his price.

On the same trip, Roni didn't heed our warning that jalapeños were lethal. He stuffed a whole one in his mouth and refused to let on he was burning up when he swallowed it. He did grab for the Coke, sputtered and turned crimson but assured us it was nothing.

Later I grew tired of the border frenzy and only returned to Mexico to take visitors or to go on my drug run. When Tsatska, our Lab, began to limp, we thought she had injured her leg after one of her perpetual ballet leaps on the patio wall. She always jumped high to see what was on the other side. But as it happens, she didn't injure her leg—Valley Fever did. I had no idea dogs could have this disease. Didn't know what it was until Diane got it the first year we were in Tucson. It is a respiratory disease in humans, treated only with rest, food, and vitamins. It causes dogs' bones to separate. A very expensive medication was prescribed for her to take continuously until she died. It was a third of the U.S. price in Mexico so of course that's where I got it. I discovered there were more pharmacies than anything else in Nogales, and they were doing a land office business—not just for dogs. A steady stream of people who had little or no drug coverage went to Mexico for their medication. It was all considerably cheaper there. When Tsatska died, the drug runs stopped, and so did the trips to Mexico.

CHAPTER 30

THAT WAGON

"Do we have everything? Are we all here? Are we ready to go? Then let's do it!"

Sol, the four younger kids, and I piled into our newly acquired Studebaker station wagon. We'd done no test drive in advance of buying it because we were in a hurry to hit the road. A trip through the desert in the summer, even at night, required limb-stretching room and the most optimal air circulation possible. And Scott had our comfy, homey, friendly, nine-passenger Ford wagon with him on the Northern Arizona University campus. That car had been our "highway home"—as close as we could get to an RV—when we pulled up roots and went west from Buffalo to Tucson. It was nearing the 100,000-mile mark, and we couldn't bear to part with it, so we kept it in the family until Scott turned over the next 100,000 miles.

This new wagon was ugly! A two-tone—brown and beige, of all colors—a box with a window in the ceiling but no A/C! We bought it from a colleague of mine who collected cars—mostly Cadillacs. I don't know how the

Studebaker muscled in on the act, but there it was, at a price we couldn't ignore. I never cared much for the owner, and a bit of that feeling may have slopped over onto the car. I hated it. I figured if it just got us to our destination and back, we could sell it and get a far more personable vehicle.

Our plan was to blaze a trail through the desert from Tucson to L.A., with Disneyland as our final goal. It is said that the desert gets cold at night. Don't believe it. That stretch of desert between Yuma and the petticoats of L.A. was brutal—even with wet cloths in the open windows and ice and water. We dripped, radiated heat, and tried to unstick our clothes, which was as successful as getting air from that little window in the ceiling. We'd have traded that window in a flash for an A/C given half a chance.

We slithered and slid our way out of the car at our host's, Cousin Don's house, and were delighted when he took us to our quarters in Redondo Beach. We had two adjoining kitchenette motel rooms with all the appropriate accouterments. We hit the showers, the pool, and the ocean as soon as we could manage—any water of the non-sweat variety was ideal. Resuscitated, we did Disneyland, and it was fun. It was our first time on the West Coast, so we took in as much as possible.

On Saturday night, we went to Hollywood and Vine—vertically—up a steep hill with a stop sign at the top, the kind Bill Cosby describes so charmingly. We were perhaps three cars from the corner when we could no longer see what was in front of us. A thick, impenetrable cloud accompanied by a most unpleasant stench suddenly surrounded us. Sol ordered us out of the car quick, fast, pronto! We complied happily. Then we saw an unending line up of cars behind us—all waiting for us to move on. We couldn't. The clutch was burned out. Don directed the unhappy folks to make way so we could glide backward down the hill. That is, so Sol could glide—we chose to walk. With the cooperation of the hapless folks behind us, Sol and Don did a remarkable job of descending the hill and coasting right into a service station at the bottom, where they promised to replace the clutch the following day.

We had an uneasy, tense, but successful ride back to Tucson, and we not only unpacked but unloaded the rotten Studebaker in short order. Some said we should have held onto it because it would be a classic. Not on your life, said I! Of course I was wrong—it became a classic—but not in time for me.

CHAPTER 31

LOST IN AN INDOOR PARKING RAMP

We were lost in an indoor parking ramp! Unbelievable, but true! It was a rainy day in Sacramento, and I was taking Diane to her clinic appointment in my rental car. I am directionally challenged, so Di was the navigator, and we arrived at the clinic promptly without incident and on time. Amazing! More amazing than that, there was no wait. The appointment took place as scheduled, and we were through in short order. Back to the parking ramp and the dilemma! Which car was our rental? On which of the three levels had we parked? We hadn't a clue. We couldn't remember the make of the car, to say nothing of the color. We began repetitive climbs, up three levels, down three levels, once, twice, three times. Nothing! Di took charge. "Stand right here and don't move," she instructed. "I'll find it, then I'll come back for you." She should have known better. I wasn't going to stay put for very long, and I didn't. Up, down, up, down, like a teeter-totter, and still nothing. Suddenly came the dawn! Rental cars always had license plate numbers attached to the keys, and they'd been in my possession all along. Sure enough, the number was there, so I took off again, this time with unabiding confidence. And there was the car right where we left it! But where was Diane?

One obstacle down, one to go. I got in the car, started the motor, and carried on with my search, which had narrowed to one thing: Diane. Up, down, up, down, no Diane. I continued cruising on all levels. Nada. I opened the windows and began calling her name, but still no response. I asked the attendants at the two exits to keep an eye out for my lost daughter, to detain her—to tell her, in General McArthur's words, "I shall return." They asked for her description! Ye Gods, I'm really bad at that! "She is about 5'8", I said, "slender, pretty, with dark brown hair and eyes." What was she wearing? I hadn't the foggiest. Probably jeans and some type of shirt and, oh yes, the baseball cap. "She's wearing a baseball cap." Still no Diane. A half-hour passed; panic set in. She is attractive, used to model, so I pictured her assaulted, shoved under a car, bashed and bloodied. I drove with eyes glued to the undersides of all vehicles. Still nothing. In desperation, I decided to leave the ramp, find a phone, call Toby to see if she had a message from Di suggesting where I could meet her.

As I headed in the direction of an exit, I heard a voice faintly calling an elongated, "Maaaaaaaaaaaaaahhhhhhhhmmm." And there she was, flanked on both sides by law enforcement. If you substitute for "attractive" "old and frail," her description to the officers of how I looked then was as inadequate as mine of her. She depicted me as a little, old, white-haired lady with a cane wearing a red jacket. She couldn't understand how my jacket had turned white. I had to remove it after working up a sweat with all that exercise and agitation. It's a smart mother who can describe her own daughter and vice versa. And she had the same scary thoughts as mine. Her search was also underneath the cars. But she was smarter. She'd had the presence of mind to contact emergency personnel, thus the male and female officers who had been shouting "Mrs. Fisher!" as Diane alternated between "Mom!" and "Irma!"

Once settled in the car, we doubled up with laughter. We got a thumbs-up from the attendant at the exit after he peered carefully into the car to see what this lost daughter really looked like. We met an irritated Toby at the soggy school grounds as she was putting her niece Taylor's bike into her car. Interrupted in her painting as she was trying to meet a deadline, she dropped everything to collect distraught Taylor, whose mom, Diane, and grandma, Irma, were supposed to get her, but didn't make it quite on time.

CHAPTER 32

DON'T WORRY BUT...

In the ignorance of youth, I thought that, when my sweet little grandmother said, "Little children, little problems—big children, big problems," the old lady didn't know what she was talking about. With the passing of time and the introduction to the three little words that strike terror into the hearts of all parents—"Don't worry but"—I realized the wisdom of grandma's statement. It began with a late-afternoon call:

"Mrs. Fisher, this is Dr. Levin from Good Samaritan Hospital in Phoenix. *Don't worry but* your daughter, Diane, was brought in this afternoon complaining of severe abdominal pains. I have kept her under observation and, while it's possible she could have had an appendicitis attack, it doesn't appear of concern at the moment. The bus taking the junior high school swim team back to Tucson is leaving in a half-hour. Do you want us to keep your daughter here so you can come and get her, or do you want her to go back on the bus?"

It would take two hours plus to get to the hospital, and another two hours to get Diane back home. After I spoke to her and learned she "felt fine now" and wanted to return with her teammates, and after I was assured by the coach that the team would be comfortable having her drive back with them, that's what she did. The two hours seemed like a millennium. When she arrived, she was tired but otherwise in good condition, both physically and emotionally—and she continued to have her appendix thirty-plus years later. The incident was, to her, an adventure.

Next came the call at 1:30 am: "Mrs. Fisher, this is Officer Calhoun from the Tucson Police Department. *Don't worry but* we were called to break up a party where minors were drinking and creating a disruption. Your daughter, Toby, was among the young people. Do you want to come to get her, or do you want her date to take her home? She will have to come to the Juvenile Court on Monday."

Amazed, I exclaimed: "At Judge Wye's house? He's notorious for being the strictest disciplinarian of minors on the circuit! How is this possible?"

"The judge is out of town and his son arranged the party without his knowledge. The judge is on his way home."

"Have my daughter or her date been drinking or causing disruption?"

"No, but they are here in the presence of others who have."

"Can you think of any reason her date shouldn't bring her home?"

"No, I can't."

Toby returned, righteously indignant, saying she and her date knew they were doing nothing wrong, which was why they didn't run out when the police came, as others had done. When they finished their game of pool, the officer said their parents had to be called and they would have to go to juvie on Monday. She was incensed and worried. I assured her the trip to the JPD would be an admonishment. No minor is supposed to remain in a situation that may be harmful. The court appearance was not what was upsetting her.

"Mom, Judge Wye didn't know John arranged the party, and now he does know, and he's going to kill him!"

No homicide took place, but John might have preferred it to whatever punishment his stern father meted out.

Later, there was the time when I was at work and my secretary buzzed me with the message that I had a call on line 3 and it sounded important.

"Mrs. Fisher, this is Dr. Wright at St. Mary's Hospital. *Don't worry but* your daughter, Debbie, was in an automobile accident. She's bruised and upset, but she'll be all right. Can you come over here?"

I dropped the phone, picked up my purse and car keys, called to my secretary to postpone my appointments, and fled the office. The ten-minute drive to the hospital took a hundred years, and so did the five-minute walk to Emergency.

My daughter, Debbie—where?"

The nurse pointed, and there she was, lying on a gurney; her hair, matted in blood, was splayed across the pillow, an Elizabethan-looking collar was around her neck, and she was immobile, sobbing, only her eyes moving. Frozen to the spot, horrified, I thought, "She's paralyzed!" The nurse, bless her, seeing my panic, told me in a calm voice that she could move but was afraid to do so. When I asked Debbie if she was in pain and told her the doctor said she would be all right, she was still inconsolable.

"But, Mom, I totaled Toby's car" she wailed. "Now what is she going to do?"

"She's going to be very happy that her sister came out of the wreck okay!"

And she was.

Finally, at 9 a.m. on a Friday, only three weeks before Debbie's wedding, a call came from my first born and only son, Scott, 52 at the time. I thought he was surprising me with a visit, which he did on occasion, but instead he said, *"Don't worry but* I am not at work." He was in the Los Alamos hospital at the urging of his colleagues. He was sure it was nothing—just indigestion. He said they were making a big deal out of it simply because he had chest pains, had pains in his arm, was short of breath, and sweated a lot. The doctor in Los Alamos took some tests but decided he needed an angiogram and wanted him to go to the hospital in Albuquerque, where they had more sophisticated equipment. He was fine he insisted. He called only to allay any fears I might have when I tried to reach him and did not find him at home or learned he was in the hospital. Not to worry, he insisted—he would keep me informed from Albuquerque. Do not come. There was no need.

Can't be a heart attack much as it sounds like it—he's too young, takes good care of himself, exercises, eats right . . . can't be! I called the airlines, and my friend in Albuquerque, and arranged with the kennel to care for my dog. I notified a couple of daughters about what happened and what I was doing, knowing the family grapevine would disseminate it almost as soon as the words were out, assured them I would phone with the results of the angiogram.

Got to the Albuquerque hospital before Scott did—his ambulance was hung up in traffic.

"What are you doing here? You didn't have to come."

I didn't waste my time trying to explain why he was wrong.

When the test was finished, the doctor informed us that surgery was indicated, a triple bypass. This was

Saturday, and it wasn't urgent enough to do on Sunday, so it would be scheduled for Monday.

I notified his sisters, who didn't ask if they should come, but just came. Two daughters and a son-in-law drove up from Tucson, two daughters and a son-in-law-to-be drove across from Denver, and one daughter flew in from Sacramento. When he saw them, his fear and anger lashed out at them and me.

To the sisters: "Why are you all here? To watch me die?"

To me: "It's all your fault! It's in the genes!"

The long, anxious wait for the result of surgery—wanting to know and not wanting to know—was hard. It was much easier sharing it with my children. We caught up with what everyone was doing, played games, and were entertained by Diane with her marvelous facility for turning ordeals into something humorous. Had a lot of laughs between tears but were ever aware of the comings and goings of each nurse, doctor, orderly, and any other hospital staff.

We stayed until we felt he would be okay and he enjoyed his five sisters in spite of himself. He was able to go home in a matter of days—less than a week—astonishing. With the help of sister Susan and her husband, Bill, we settled him in his home in Santa Fe, and got him on a routine.

Then, about three weeks later, we met him at the airport in Denver as we all gathered for Debbie's wedding. A little thinner, moving a bit more slowly and carefully, he danced and joined in every festivity to the joy, relief, and delight of us all—and all included all my children and all my grandchildren. It was a blessing!

Here is the riddle. When is a child no longer a child? My brother said at our father's deathbed that we were orphans now, no longer children. We became the venerable ones. So the answer is that a child is a child until his parents die. *Don't worry but* he will survive and be strong until his time comes. And so it goes, from generation to generation. That's life.

CHAPTER 33

THE MEN IN MY DAUGHTERS' LIVES

Number-one daughter's man was Dan. The first, he broke all the barriers, paving the way for the ones who

followed. He was a good-looking soldier stationed in our town, with a multitude of strikes against him. Major for me was he came, of all places, from the South—a small town in Alabama. Major for Sol was that he wasn't Jewish. I wasn't overjoyed that he was from so fundamentalist a religion as the

Dan Newman

Church of Christ, but I believed in what I preached to my kids—if you are a good, whatever religion you are, it's all one and the same. To me, the basic tenets of all religions follow the golden rule; just the trappings are different. Dan volunteered to convert, but he would fear on his deathbed he would go to "Hell and damnation." Then don't, I told him. I had never broached the subject with him, never expected him to convert, never would have asked that of him.

He wasn't sure what he was going to be when he got out of service (at least he wasn't regular military) but he was thinking of law enforcement in his hometown, like one of his uncles. What a combination! A fundamentalist, bigoted, redneck, I thought in my own bigoted way. I hadn't yet gotten over my horrendous experience of living in the Southland during the Second World War.

He said he'd never heard of the KKK, a likely story. "Impossible!" said I. He feigned total ignorance of what it was. We pulled out the encyclopedia and showed him articles on the KKK before he would allow there might be such a thing. His protestations were true, as it turned out. He really *didn't* know anything about it. After being mustered out of service and visiting back home, he returned to town. He confessed to us, in a mild state of shock, that all the male members of his family belonged to the KKK, which they called a club, and that's what he thought it was. He attended one of their meetings and was distressed by it. That won him some brownie points.

So he became a cop in our town and turned into one of the good guys. We ended up on some of the same committees at work, and I found that the bigoted,

judgmental remarks he'd made in my presence were just
to raise my ire. Our thinking was actually down the same
line, the right line, my line. He became the life of the party
at the Seder dinners and grew to like gefilte fish, which I
understand he keeps in his refrigerator. There was another
side to him, which was not very agreeable. That side I did
not see, but my daughter did, and she found it so
unpleasant she divorced him after two sons, a daughter,
and fifteen years of marriage.

Many years passed, and then another Dan came
upon the scene. An orthopedic surgeon, married and
divorced three times. He was a spoiled-rotten rich kid
who acted like the king of the hill. He was controlling, had
a terrible temper, was intimidating. That marriage lasted
one year, which seemed a very long year, and was a relief
when it was over.

Then came number-two daughter's man, David,
the hunter and ball player. He and my daughter went to
high school together. Another good-looking guy, he was a
mix of Mexican American, Anglo, and Creek Indian. We
thought he was Catholic; we bought into the stereotypical
concept that all Mexican Americans were. He wasn't. He

was Episcopalian. Is there such a thing as a lax or relaxed Episcopalian? If so, he was it. He was interested and comfortable learning the Jewish customs and participating in the few traditions we relaxed Jews entertained.

We learned the stress and strain of having a ball player in the family. The baseball games I used to enjoy were tense now. What if he missed a catch as short stop or made an error? We sweated out his turn at bat until he made a hit or an out and ended the agony—until his next time up. It was no longer a fun, exciting game. It was a living. When he was cut

David Jacome

from the game, he took it philosophically and turned to graphic art, which had been his major in college. Hunting, with which we had absolutely no experience, was his prime priority even when his wife was just days from delivering their first child. Jewish entertainment is bridge, golf, tennis, eating, but never—or rarely ever—hunting.

His mother and a high school math teacher said he was an underachiever. He probably was. He had the stereotypical Mexican American attitude—man makes the living, woman takes care of kids, husband, and home. The problem was he didn't make a living and was opposed to his wife doing so. This, among other things—such as the complete disparity between their philosophies of life—caused the wife to divorce him after three sons and six years of marriage.

Third daughter's handsome, well-mannered, well-spoken gentleman Tracy from New Jersey was next on

Tracy Eddinger

the scene. A high-class, efficient waiter in a high-class restaurant. His charm and solicitousness held him in good stead. It was an amazement to see and hear this soft-spoken, mild-mannered man bark out

orders in clipped tones to some co-workers who helped serve at their wedding dinner. It was further amazing to see how well they accepted and respected him. A compassionate and generous man, he seemed to have an endless supply of money. Some indicators and a lot of speculation regarding the hard-to-detect source made us uneasy. Due to irreconcilable differences, they divorced amicably after one year of marriage. They remained good and caring friends.

Then, out of the blue, appeared Roger, who fathered the third daughter's daughter. He is tall, slender, blonde, Nordic looking, and another artist. He designs and manufactures clothes

Roger Alan

in San Francisco for women and men, particularly sport clothes. His most significant contribution was to collaborate in the making of the most marvelous young girl ever. Mother, father, and child were together for the first six months of her life after which the parents, who were incompatible, separated. They maintained contact always because of the wonder child they had in common.

And then there was Bob, a very significant man in number-three daughter's life. Her daughter called him her

Bod Hirsh

stepfather although they'd never married and didn't live together. He is a competent, successful criminal defense attorney, who insists all his clients are innocent—at least in his eyes. He makes them a part of his family while he represents them, which probably contributes to his record of wins. He appears absent-minded, is a talker, seldom seems to listen, and he creates clutter all around him. His action in court markedly contrasts with this behavior. Without referring to a note, he questions witnesses in an organized, direct, superbly efficient manner. He is physically active, rides the rapids on the Colorado River, and skis on water and snow. He was a compassionate, caring friend to Diane and Taylor and an integral part of their lives. He and Diane had an ongoing close relationship, which had been sustained for ten years.

Finally there was Les, a sweet, loving man who put up with her mood swings due to being bipolar. He stood by her through her fun, caring, good times and patiently hung in there during her nasty, very difficult bad times. He played

Les Brown and Diane

lovely and loving ballads he wrote about her and for her and sang them to her. He made her last days far better than anyone could imagine.

Next came number-four daughter's Bill. It is my considered opinion that he is really of my generation and was frozen and thawed out just in time for my gal. He knows every oldie and goodie from my time, even as far back as the '30s. He said he learned them from his mother as she bounced him on her knee. He learned carpentry from his father, uses it as needed in his own home, wanted it as his occupation, but the bottom dropped out of the market so he went back to school and into something else. Graphic art was his bag, as were and still

Bill Mrosek

are the inner workings of computers. He is an inordinate help in he his wife's greeting-card business. He's energetic, a doer, was among the student protestors against the Vietnam War in the Nixon era, as was seen full face on the TV news at the time.

He plays the guitar, sings with a band, does a great karaoke job with Mac the Knife and dances up a storm. He dotes on his wife, which gives him zillions of brownie points from me. They decided early on not to have kids, which is just as well. He'd be a pain in the neck mid-Victorian dad if they had a daughter. He's been in the family thirty-seven years now. He's definitely a keeper. He has to be. I've made it clear to the children that they can do whatever they please with me when I die, but I want them to be a hundred percent sure I'm dead before they do anything. He's the guy who immediately came to the fore and assured me he would take care of it. He promised he'd drive a wooden spike through my heart, so he has to stay around because I know I can count on him.

Fifth daughter's Barry was next on the hit parade. A lean, lanky cowboy type who worked for the university's museum studying tree rings and the like, then moved to computer support and Training at the University. He plucks a mean guitar and plays the steel pedal and bass guitar and sings in the same band as Bill. He has an impressive amount of amplifying and recording equipment. Very much a homeboy, he is

Barry Richards

comfortable and happy in his niche. His preference was not to venture forth beyond the limited boundaries he set for himself. This did not jive with the pace and direction of his upwardly mobile, eager-to-explore-the-world wife. No children, by mutual agreement, they amicably divorced after twelve years of marriage.

And then came number-two Bill, who came into her life fifteen years ago. He is a multi-talented man, or should I say a man of multitudinous interests. He likes to fish, scuba dive, ski and hike and he plays the drums like Gene Krupa. He is an artist who carves birds and paints beautiful, realistic pictures of wildlife.

Bill Alther

He got his degree in wildlife biology and worked at the Museum of Natural History. He ultimately resigned from that job and gave full time to his art, which is magnificent.

He also does marvelous things with wood, like rebuilding the steps in his house, the cabinetry in the kitchen and bathrooms, and a screen for the living room. He is a perfectionist who agonizes over making "major" decisions—like which shade of what color to use on the wall—which tries everyone's patience, but the finished product is always magnificent. And he lives a good portion of his life in Andy Griffith's Mayberry, USA.

These significant men in my daughters' lives became, by default, a big part of mine. They deserve and receive honorable mention in my memoirs.

PART FIVE

FOR BETTER OR WORSE

CHAPTER 34

LET 'EM ROLL

Our good times after the kids were down for the night fell into two categories, "ongoing" and "special events." Ongoing were the duplicate bridge games, our study group, dance classes and get-away weekends. Bridge met once every two weeks or once a month, can't remember which, and was comprised of twelve people, six couples, making up three tables. We took turns playing at one another's

Dave and Lucille, dancers and bridge players.

homes, and served soft drinks, "nasharie," and dessert. The games were fun, unlike some of the tense, serious types that I have been in since. Everyone showed up religiously or sent substitutes. The only time I remember a game being disrupted was when one of our members, a veterinarian, had an emergency call about a goldfish that was drowning. We thought it was a joke, that he was putting us on. We asked if he was going to give mouth-to-mouth resuscitation. He was dead serious and angry at our insensitive reactions. Later, we apologized profusely.

About the same number but not all of the same people made up our study group. I think we met once a month, and again, we took turns going from one home to another. Our agenda was flexible. If there was a subject or issue that troubled or interested a majority of us, we either invited someone knowledgeable in the field to speak to us or one or more of our members would do the research and present it at the next meeting. The topics selected were as far-flung as the differences in our membership. The group consisted of engineers, lawyers, doctors, businessmen, teachers, and housewives (being a housewife was not a noble profession in those days). Being Jewish was our only common denominator, and that was not by design. It did make it challenging for the priest who explained the virgin birth and the trinity in a multitude of ways until he finally threw up his hands and said, "Either you believe or you don't believe"—which became his final answer.

Our monthly dance classes were not in the fox trot or waltz, but the samba, the mamba, the rumba, and the cha-cha-cha. We stepped to the radio or record music in our nightclub-style basement with its milk bar and dance floor surrounded by booths. We were a swinging crew, and we made the whole house rock. It was lots of fun.

As Sol and I added more children to our family, we were tied down to increasingly stringent routines, so periodic escapes were essential to our well-being. Sol and I began taking quarterly romantic weekends away from home, just the two of us, but not far away. We stayed in the hotels in Buffalo, then bravely ventured out to Niagara Falls, Canada. We were awakened on one of our trips to the falls by a cacophony of bells that we could feel as well as hear. The noise was so loud we couldn't tell what one another said, even though we were side by side in bed. We figured it would only last a minute or two, or five at the outside. No way! This earsplitting racket went on for more than fifteen minutes, subsided for about the same length of time, then started all over again. We later learned it was to honor the Queen of England, who had just arrived for a royal visit. We continued our great escapes when we moved to Tucson, staying in motels, dude ranches, or hotels in and around town. On very special occasions we went to beautiful Sedona, Arizona. It was a marvelous way to maintain our sanity. I heartily recommend it.

The special events were trips with our friends, with or without the children. Toured Fort Niagara in Canada with the Friedman family, where adults and children alike were impressed by the fort itself and the guards with all their accoutrement, dressed in their colorful uniforms. Rode bicycles built for two, swam in

Irma and Betty at Bemus Point.

Sol and Irma riding tandem— Bemus Point.

mud-bottom Lake Chataqua, and stayed in cabins at Bemus Point.

We dined, danced, and fished at Lake Muskoka in Canada with the Fudemans. Sol admonished Betty and me to stop our incessant chatter, informing us that fishermen were silent so as not to scare the fish off. He was the only one to catch a fish.

We had an unforgettable trip to the Neville in the Catskills, where cousin Bill was the star performer, not by design. One of the highlights of our action-packed week of entertainment was the hypnotist. Bill looked forward to that stellar event, though he put no stock in its validity.

**Top: waiter, dance teachers, Irma, Sol, waiter
Bottom: Bill, Arlene, Betty, Dave (Nevelle)**

When the day finally came, the hypnotist began by casting his spell over the audience in general. Those who "went under" were called to the stage, and lo and behold, Bill was among them. Since he was a professional actor, we thought he was putting us on by going up on the stage. He followed all the hypnotist's orders, including eating a lemon. He did so with relish. It was at this point that his wife, Arlene, told us with great surprise and conviction that he really was "under." She said he *couldn't*, not just *wouldn't*, eat a lemon at all unless he were under a spell of some sort. She was convinced! Then the hypnotist told him and three others that they were at a horse race and should hurry to place their bets. The race was about to begin. The hypnotist named their horses, and Bill's was "A Be Gezundt." Bill shouted his horse on with such verve that it won. He was then surreptitiously told to collect on his bet but to be careful nobody saw how much he was getting or he might be mugged. He was given a fist full of newspaper cut to dollar-bill size and told to put it quickly and secretly in his inside left jacket pocket, which he did. When it was all over and he rejoined us he was exasperated to learn he had missed the whole performance. He didn't believe us when we told him he *was* the performance until we asked him to look in his jacket pocket. He was pissed!

One year, we should have gone to Las Vegas because we were winners in two separate events; we were on a roll. We won a fifty-pound sack of potatoes at a PTA meeting and a bottle of champagne in a waltz contest. We were versatile—at least our winnings were—as they went from the plebeian to the ritzy.

We had marvelous times on our cruises. We celebrated our fifteenth wedding anniversary on the Great Lakes cruise to the Mackinaw Islands. It was lovely, quiet (not even the sound of birds because of the

spray they inflicted on the island to make it allergy free), and no cars. We were carted around in little man-drawn carriages. The hotel room was lovely, like a bridal suite. I thought of it as our delayed honeymoon.

We celebrated our fortieth anniversary on the Caribbean cruise on the Carnival Line. I thought we were being invaded by aliens from outer space because so many of the passengers had little circles of something behind their ears. I had never seen or heard of this method of preventing seasickness. I never had the need of it. There

were activities around the clock and food beautifully and generously presented everywhere all the time, including the Grand Gala Buffet

from 12:30 to 1:30 a.m.! It was so plentiful and accessible that I ate less than I otherwise would.

We played shuffleboard and ping-pong and danced in the many different halls, each with its special kind of music. When I swam in the pool on deck, I discovered to my distasteful surprise that it was filled with ocean water. The heavy salt content in the mouthful I swallowed was a rude awakening! I won seventy dollars in a Bingo game, which Sol tried to con me out of so he could use it to gamble in the casino. I was tough. I held onto it, which is why I can say with a certainty that I *won* seventy bucks. Of course we helped the economy at our tourist stops by leaving money in each shop.

We drank in the cool ocean breeze when we walked around the decks. We were mesmerized as we sat in our deck chairs watching the movement of the water and the stars filling the sky as the sun went down. It was hard to return to the real world after being pampered. At home we didn't have the chocolate candy on doilies on our pillows or the bed turned down. Those were the good old days!

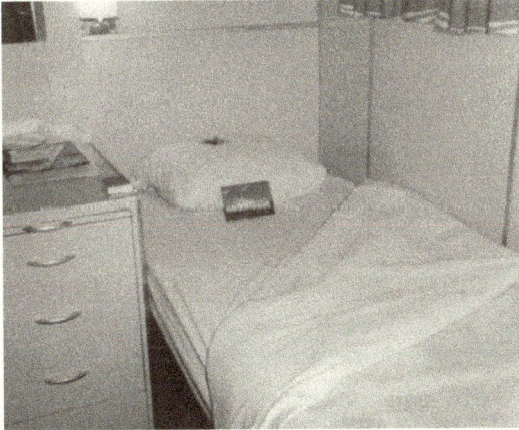

Chapter 35

SIEGE

"Turn over, you're snoring!"

Thank God! That's better. Three-ten in the morning. There's still time to get some sleep

Sudden snoring . . . roaring . . . amplified . . . volume increased . . . tempo increased . . . faster . . . faster . . . frantic. Arms flailing . . . legs thrashing . . . body convulsing.

"Wake up! . . . What's wrong? . . . Wake up! . . . Oh my God!"

Body convulsing . . . arches back . . . stiff . . . very stiff . . . head flung back . . . eyes rolling . . . whites showing . . . then . . . collapse . . . silent . . . still . . . very silent . . . very still . . . too silent . . . too still.

No response to voice or touch. Is he breathing? Can't hear his heart beat in his chest. Can't get a pulse! Not in his wrist. Not in his throat. Not in his ankle. No response, no matter what. No movement . . . frighteningly still. Call 911 . . . where's the phone . . . get hold of yourself . . . can't speak if you keep gulping air . . . must breath . . . must speak.

"Hello, hello . . . ? Please help . . . we need help. What? The problem? Something is terribly wrong with my husband. He won't respond to me. I can't get a pulse. I don't think he's breathing . . . "

Questions—lots of questions—name—address—phone number.

"Who else is in the house? Two children, sleeping." "Animals? Yes, two dogs. Put them out? Yes. Door locked? Yes. Light on? No. Turn light on . . . unlock door . . . Yes, but please hurry. No, he hasn't moved, hasn't changed at all. Still won't answer me . . . won't wake up!

"I think I hear them . . . yes, two men running, still pulling their clothes on . . . they're here! Thanks, operator."

"In here. No, no change." More questions. What doctor? . . . What hospital? . . . Happened before? . . . On medication?

Another man comes in, a cop. Oxygen, tubes, wires, syringes, so much equipment, so much activity . . . blood pressure, EKG, pulse, temperature . . . Talk, lots of talk, to one another, over the radio, on the phone . . . two more men . . . ambulance drivers . . . everyone crowded around the bed . . . very little room for me . . . children peering from their bedroom doorway, terrified . . . my fear barks at them, "Close the door—get back to sleep."

Someone says he's coming out of it? Look out . . . let me see. Let me get close enough to see. His eyes open. He's startled . . . sees the five men crowded around the bed. Looks for me . . . at me . . . angry . . . erupts . . .

"What did you do?!"

I'm choked up, can't speak. . . . He isn't dead! . . . Breathless, weak, can't respond . . . too much to take in . . . thank God he isn't dead. The paramedics tell him what happened . . . he remembers nothing. Someone says hospital . . . tests . . . check-up . . . find out what happened. He's arguing . . . nothing wrong with him . . . they convince him as they load him on the gurney.

"Meet us there?" they ask me.

"Soon as I get dressed."

The children . . . have to tell them . . . tell them I'll call from the hospital as soon as I know what's happening.

He's in an emergency room, rested, comfortable in bed, joking, laughing with the nurses and paramedics.

Asks why I made such a big fuss . . . not necessary . . . no, he still remembers nothing. He'll go through the tests to satisfy everyone else, but it's not necessary . . . nothing wrong with him . . . just a fluke. Pricking, poking, attaching him to machines, tests, tests, and more tests . . . nothing conclusive. Want to keep him overnight to watch . . . monitor him. No way he'll agree.

"Nothing wrong with me. Have to pick up my in-laws from the airport this afternoon. Can't stay here. Waste of time."

They capitulate.

"See your regular doctor . . . next three days . . . follow up . . . he'll tell you what has to be done. Meantime, take it easy."

Take it easy! Easier to stop the water flowing at Niagara Falls or to stop Mt. Etna in the midst of a volcanic eruption.

Intense relief! He motor-mouths all the way home, outlining what he has to do, what I have to do, what the children have to do before we get my parents. "And don't say anything to them about me . . . no need to worry them . . . it was nothing."

And everything was done in time, and we picked up my parents and the doctors reached no conclusion . . . until years later. And I never again had an easy night's sleep as long as he was lying beside me. . . . Never . . . not ever!

CHAPTER 36

TRAGEDY

Early on, it was fun to discuss things with Sol. There were stimulating debates, challenging, parrying back and forth in equal time and with good humor. He loved to play the devil's advocate, taking either side to enliven the exchange and broaden the thinking. Then, without a clue, imperceptibly, this exceptionally strong, healthy man became ill. The change was so slow at the start that it was virtually unrecognizable. The physical difficulties were the easiest and quickest to perceive. Numbness in his hands that made buttoning and unbuttoning impossible and necessitated a mug to be held in two hands because in one it would crash to the floor. Then came the dizziness, imbalance, fatigue, double vision, headaches, and more. Gradually, cognitive and perceptual problems loomed. Turning an undershirt this way and that, over and over, trying to find a plan of attack to finally get it on! Straight lines became jagged. His exceptional skill at math failed him. Simple number problems, even balancing the checkbook, were beyond him. Instead of sitting on top of his world as always, he was falling into a frightening abyss without a safety net. He was losing control and he couldn't abide it. And we didn't see it. We were busy addressing the symptoms, surviving.

There were some signs. But there was the urgent need to cope quickly. The creditors were dunning us, his job was tenuous, and the demands of our growing children required an ever-increasing income. The reins were slipping from his hands and they had to be grasped and retained by someone, by me, as our family's world was fragmenting.

Our frantic effort to regain balance kept us from recognizing clues or understanding their significance. He changed from devil's advocate to becoming the devil himself. He offended, denigrated, demeaned, belittled, irritated, angered, and enraged people. The victims of his abuse were those over whom he brandished authority: his children and his employees and persons not as articulate as he.

When our family stabilized and time allowed for reflection, the reason behind his unacceptable conduct was finally identified, and help was offered. It was too late. The pattern of his behavior was firmly entrenched, and so was his refusal to do anything to alter it. To hang on, to pull himself up, he felt he had to push others down. Sol was strong, and he pushed with all his might; he pushed so hard and insensitively that he pushed everyone away from him forevermore.

CHAPTER 37

THE STRANGER

Our Adonis, strong and mighty,
Vibrant, virile, vital,
Challenging, exciting, stimulating,
Swift, sure, steady, solid.

Our protector, who wrapped us in his cloak
Of comfort and safety,
Our shield, our rock, our love.

Was slowly stolen away,
Edged away, little by little,
Deceptively, imperceptibly,
Stealthily, sneakily, horrifically.

Was seized, abducted, was gone,
Disappeared, vanished,
Ceased to exist.

Was replaced, an adult changeling,
By a fearsome, evil, incestuous stranger
With an oily sneer, a cutting tongue,
Denigrating, excoriating.

Who wrapped the cloak too tightly,
Suffocating, choking, strangling.
Irritating, exasperating, infuriating,
Heartbreaking.

Walked in the same body,
But clumsily, cumbersomely.
Looked out through the same eyes,

But contemptuously,
Greedily, leeringly.

This duplicitous, perfidious,
Treacherous stranger
Who pretended to be
My husband.

CHAPTER 38

MORNIN GLORY

It was at this most difficult time in my life that I met Mornin Glory who demanded the most from me, got it and gave it. Sol was diagnosed with multiple sclerosis, our six children were still dependent, I had to become "gainfully employed." My total work experience was two weeks at Halle Brothers in Cleveland! I "filled in" in the toiletries department while I was an undergraduate at Western

Mornin Glory

Reserve University, as it was called in the dark ages. The State Welfare Department had an opening for a social worker, my second choice of a career, the first being marriage and a family. My bachelor's degree qualified me. Applying for the job was embarrassing because of the paucity of information I was able to put on the application form. The oral interview by a panel of formidable strangers was terrifying!

That was where I first met Mornin, one of the panel members. They already had my vital statistics: age, race, religion, marital status, children, and education. Those questions were legal in the olden days. That was the easy part. Telling why I wanted the job was not too difficult either. The hard part was describing what I would bring to Family and Children's Services. Mornin led me through it with grace, flair and easy facility. Due to her skill, I got the job, and then found, to my happy surprise, that she was to be my supervisor.

Mornin was the best thing that could happen to a forty-three-year-old, tense, anxiety-ridden, and totally inexperienced novice. She was not just an able social worker but a challenging, demanding, creative supervisor. A black woman of my age, brought up in the hills of West Virginia, she rose through the ranks to the level of regional district supervisor in Children's Social Services. Her advancement in position was accomplished against odds that would have daunted a less gutsy person. It was necessary to cover a large area in her work, which resulted in her having to be away a number of days at a time. Following the custom of social workers traveling in pairs, her partner registered for the "white only" hotel room while she entered through the window. It was during the '50s and '60s, when segregation was at high tilt. It was then that she developed her habit of carrying very large handbags (her substitute suitcases), which she continued all of her days.

She looked a lot like Pearl Bailey when they were both in the young, slim mode—even their mannerisms were similar. Her long, slender, beautiful fingers were hard to miss, since much of her emphasis when she spoke was with her hands. She liked good clothes and jewelry, wore them with pizzazz, and was always in the height of fashion if not a little ahead of it. She was tastefully flamboyant—if that's not an oxymoron. And with all her flare, she was one of the most conservative, traditional people I ever knew, especially in relation to family—hers, yours, mine.

She was inordinately agitated when she learned that my oldest daughter was going to marry a southerner from the Church of Christ.

"She's Jewish!" Episcopalian Mornin exhorted. " How can you let her do that?"

"What do you mean *let* her do that?"

When her son, the apple of her eye, married a white woman from a Jewish family I asked her how she could *let* him do that, to which she heatedly responded:

"Oh, shut up!"

Mornin, a black Episcopalian woman, made an authentic Yiddisha Momma. When a young co-worker came to work on the Jewish New Year, she admonished her.

"What are you doing here today? Go home! It's your holiday."

To which the sweet young thing replied, "But I'm not going to Temple."

To which Mornin retorted, "I don't care where you go. I want you out of here—*now*!" She left, and her father phoned Mornin later to thank her.

It was my good fortune that she'd left her job in West Virginia to follow her husband, a high school math teacher and athletic coach, to Tucson. That meant she was "on tap" when I needed her. In her unique way she imparted insights, knowledge, backbone, wisdom, almost invisibly. A Caucasian client had come to Arizona from another state, had been raped by a black man, wanted her baby placed for adoption, and Arizona allowed cross-racial placements unlike her state of origin. My coworkers mercilessly ribbed me about my gullibility.

"Raped," they chided, "Ha! A likely story!"

When the hospital notified the agency that the baby was born, Mornin, in her inimitable way, commanded, "Get out there and find out if that baby is a Nigger!"

I was horrified by her use of the "n-word" but did as she ordered. The baby was unmistakably biracial—so much for my gullibility. Happily, she was placed with a mixed couple, a black man and a white woman. Wish I could see how that sweet, bright babe turned out.

Mornin used the word "nigger" as one of her shock techniques to sensitize and desensitize us. Once she educated a group of nuns about the need to provide services to unwed fathers, not only to unwed mothers. She pantomimed a foursome of gossipy women playing cards. As she was dealing, she began the conversation:

"Have you heard about Mary? And Joseph isn't even the father!"

She got her point across, and without offending the nuns. I can't imagine anyone else getting away with that. Her methods were often disconcerting but, if you could rock with the shocks, the benefits were invaluable.

She taught, spurred all her supervisees on (with a kick in the pants if necessary), and let us vent when we overdosed with severe, seemingly and sometimes really, insoluble people problems. If we began to falter, she admonished us to "stand ten feet tall, go out and do what is necessary," and we did. She was one of a-kind, a happening. She prodded me to do things I

Mornin and son, Dave

never thought I was capable of doing. I have been everlastingly grateful to her for that. I was also fortunate that she let me into her life, for she was a very private person. We became fast friends, which was truly marvelous.

CHAPTER 39

CATACLYSM

He swam toward me. As he came close to embrace me, a piercing voice shattered the still summer's air.

"Don't touch me!" it shouted, and the voice came from me, startling me and shocking him. He quickly retreated without a word. And I felt an icy chill in the 100-plus-degree afternoon.

It was a spontaneous reaction, but it wasn't sudden. It was a culmination of months—eons—of frustration, despair, and anger. The last trigger was my daughter's distraught, anguished cry over the phone: "But I do hate him! I have a right to hate him—for molesting me for years—and not just me!" I couldn't breathe. I couldn't speak. I gasped, and she recanted, terrified. "Mom, don't say anything to him. Don't tell him I told you. Promise me or I won't speak to you again. I don't want to be responsible for you splitting up."

I promised, long enough to recoup and regroup. I'd had no idea! I had not the slightest suspicion, yet I never questioned the validity of what she told me. I believed it and then castigated myself. How could I not have known? Why didn't she, or one of the other children, tell me before? How long had this gone on? Who else was affected? How extensive was it?

Carrying on as usual was impossible, but what could I do? I had already been considering divorce and had moved out of the bedroom, but the children weren't aware of this. I hadn't even discussed divorce with Sol yet. He knew something was wrong, but he didn't know what. Neither did I. I had already taken steps to have him evaluated to see if he could live on his own. The results weren't in yet. All of this was before my frightful phone call. I had no one to talk to about what was happening. We were to leave the next week for a month in Italy, our first European trip. We were to be joined by my brother and sister-in-law. I could talk to my brother, thank God.

I wanted to see the children before leaving the country, but they wouldn't come to our house. They were all independent adults, living in their own homes, so I met with them at one of their homes. It was a tense, stressful, very difficult get together—everyone vulnerable and in shock. The daughter who had blurted the information to me had not been the only one molested, but they had never shared this knowledge with one another—and certainly not with me. They were unanimous in their desire to keep it a secret, not to be shared with their brother or to be discussed with their father, the perpetrator. They were so fragile that I had to agree to their conditions, at least until I could have some time to think—to sort things out. They wanted Sol and I to carry on, business as usual.

At this stage of our marriage, I could barely tolerate Sol, and now, with these new facts, he was completely repugnant to me.

How in the world was I going to be able to get through a full month without spewing my fury at him? My ire was not just directed at him—but even more intensely, at myself. I was only aware of his verbal abuse, which I'd tried, unsuccessfully, to deflect. I was very familiar with child molestation. Part of my work over twenty years was to detect it, to protect the children and work with their parents. I knew its devastating effects. Why didn't I see it? Why didn't I create an atmosphere that allowed the children to tell me about it? I couldn't answer my own questions, and I agonized over them.

On my arrival in Rome, I spoke to Bob, advised him about my situation, and he was appalled. I told him that, during our flight, I decided I was going to get out of my marriage, to leave Sol upon my return to the States, because to remain in this relationship was intolerable. I was determined not to share this decision with Sol or the children until my return home, when I would be better able to handle the fall-out. Bob made no effort to influence my decision one way or another but was very supportive of the conclusion I reached.

It was a relief and he was a comfort. And we returned from that wonderful country.

Sol and I separated in 1985, divorced in 1986, and the children and I spent years mending and healing. When Sol died in January of 1995, I could not mourn for him. My mourning for him had begun in 1965 and finally ended twenty years later.

CHAPTER 40

THE DIVORCE

A week after our forty-third wedding anniversary, our divorce became final. Although it could hardly be considered an impulsive or capricious move after all that time, my former friends exhorted, "How can you do this to that sick, old man!" My friends said, "I'm sure you had good reasons to make this difficult decision." My son said, "What took you so long?" Others said, "You could have won an academy award for making your marriage look so successful. We envied you." A therapist friend said, "You filled the holes in your husband, creating the illusion he was still the original man you married, when this was far from the truth."

The divorce was a gradual, overwhelming process, the hardest action I have ever taken in my life, but I had to do it and only wish I had done it a lot sooner. The first and most difficult hurdle in this horrendous obstacle course was to get a definitive diagnosis and prognosis of Sol's condition. As it turned out, many years were wasted by a misdiagnosis of MS. A new neurologist, who took over from the original, now deceased neurologist when he was on vacation, said directly to Sol, "I don't know what you have, but you do *not* have MS." Our primary doctor was furious with the young neurologist who fractured protocol by giving his information directly to the patient instead of to him. He refused to accept the neurologist's statement and called in a neurosurgeon, who reaffirmed the original diagnosis. More years passed before we learned that a doctor in our own community was doing research on MS. He concurred with the young neurologist. It was absolutely not MS! He put Sol through a multitude of tests, which revealed that an irregular heartbeat was preventing the blood from getting to the brain the way it should. This resulted in brain damage, which could have been reduced or minimized if it had been detected and treated earlier. Once it was discovered, the new regimen arrested the ongoing damage. However, the harm already done could not be reversed and was so deleterious to the entire family that the children left home at their first opportunity, and life for Sol and me was intolerable.

The second, most time-consuming obstacle, was breaking the shackles of tradition, sundering the commitment that was so strongly imbued in my generation—"in *sickness* and in health, 'til death do us part." Divorce was not an option in my mind, not for a very long time, much too long for the children.

The third obstacle was the need for survival, not just for me, but for the family. Providing the basic needs of food, shelter, and clothing and medical bills had been my husband's province and I was totally unprepared to assume it. Between us, we'd managed. He changed jobs to one he was able to handle for a number of years and I became "gainfully employed" until my retirement twenty years later.

Once the children were grown and out on their own, our life together became more and more nightmarish. Sol stopped work on a disability retirement and vegetated in front of the TV until I got home. He became smotheringly dependent upon me so that, once I also retired, I was almost stifled to death. Visits with the children were lessening, as were those with friends. No one wanted to be with a cantankerous man who irritated, angered, and often embarrassed them. Neither did I, but I couldn't see any alternative. I tried to encourage Sol to go for counseling, with or without me, and he absolutely refused. A friend in rehabilitation also tried, to no avail. There was no way I could broach the subject without raising his ire and getting his outraged shout: "Stop caseworking me!" A change of scenery did nothing to alter the situation, not even our trips to Israel and to Italy. They provided momentary relief, but then we returned to our almost reclusive, miserable life.

This was intolerable—something had to be done—and I had to do it. I felt sure that Sol's dependency was not healthy for either of us and I couldn't seem to break us out of its cycle. I wanted desperately to be free of him, but not to his detriment. I managed to get him in for a psychiatric work-up to learn what would happen if I left him. All but one psychiatrist said he would be able to manage all right. The one who dissented said he would commit suicide. After all my years with Sol, I could not believe he would ever do such a thing so I went ahead with plans to separate from him. I did it with fear and trepidation, but out of desperation for the survival of us all.

He begged me to wait until after our fiftieth anniversary, but that was impossible. By this time, he was repugnant to me and, after I learned he had molested the girls, I couldn't abide him at all. This was especially so because he absolutely refused to acknowledge and take responsibility for his behavior, which would have validated their feelings and helped them in the healing process.

I told him I'd found an apartment, was moving within the week because I couldn't remain in the same house with him. I wanted to affect a separation before broaching the subject of divorce. I was afraid that, if he were to contest it, a judge might not grant a divorce. Sol was, after all, a sick old man. He refused to let me move out, so I found an apartment for him that he liked, furnished it with things he enjoyed, split everything we had down the middle, and drew a long breath of relief when I returned home, alone! The mountain was off my shoulders; I could breathe freely and deeply and life was worth living again.

I took the tough-love approach, changed the locks on the doors, tolerated no contact from Sol, and it worked. He made friends with tenants in his apartment complex and modified his behavior somewhat because he had no choice. He became acclimated. After a few months, I filed for divorce, which was uncontested. We started life anew. It was better for the children and blissfully good for me. Sol died from a heart attack, not suicide, in 1995.

Hard as it was, I learned a lot from this agonizing process. After so many years, divorce is much like an amputation. Perhaps it is that way even after a few years. Old habits die hard and, sadly, the good memories shared are almost obliterated by the bad. I learned how to live single in this coupled world, that friends look different in the spotlight of divorce, that, late as it was, it is never too late, and that tough as it was, it is good. I only wish I had done it much sooner.

CHAPTER 41

GRIEVE THE LIVING

It is not my habit to dwell on the past—to think in terms of "should have" or "would have," "to cry over spilled milk" or any other clichés of like nature. However, when my children encouraged me to write my memoirs, I was pressed into reliving the past. I found that, with the distance of elapsed time, insights became visible that were not even glimpsed then. One of these is a virtually new discovery, to me at least, and it is about this that I write. It is the need for the helping professions and society to give permission to grieve for the living. A lot has been written fairly recently about grieving over a loss as in death and dying or in a divorce. But there is another type of loss that has been overlooked, which is just as important, perhaps even more so, and it needs to be addressed. It should be particularly familiar to medical social workers and doctors. The following attests to the need.

OUR STORY

Startled by the arm flung across my chest, I looked at the familiar body lying beside me. It was unbelievable how that magnificent physique remained the same as it was, filled with the excitement and comfort from the inhabitant of that body over the years—but he was no longer there. It was as though he'd left, had been forced out, abducted or destroyed. An uninvited, unwanted alien had taken over, was the new inhabitant. This transgressor vacillated between being an irascible, argumentative, oppositional, abusive demon and an exceedingly dependent, inadequate, ineffectual, nonentity or a persistently demanding, haranguing, nagging leech. Whichever form he took, he was markedly and profoundly different from the original. Sometimes the change was slow, almost unrecognizable, and at other times it was shockingly fast, a sudden trip to the Twilight Zone. But this was not science fiction. It happened in our real world. It was frightening. The earth shifted beneath our feet, the world spun and split out of the galaxy, and I felt like I was falling and there was no one there to catch me.

I was frozen into this new relationship, not of my own making, nor Sol's, nor that of anyone else. I remembered what Sol was like when we met—handsome, athletic, gregarious, with many friends—male and female—so appealing. He was bright, had been valedictorian of his high school class, excelled in math and prided himself on it. He was quick, energetic—always ran up the staircase two or three steps at a time and was always at least a half a block ahead of me when we were out walking. I never could keep up his pace—hardly anyone could. He was capable, assertive, resolutely independent, and responsible. He started working at an early age and was supporting his mother and sister when we met—then he added me and, ultimately, our six children. He was a crackerjack salesman, a good provider, holding as many jobs as it took to care for his family—often two and three at a time. How much fun it was to socialize, to entertain, and to be "people persons." We couldn't have done it if he hadn't helped with the housework and the children—doing everything: bathing, changing, feeding, playing, and reading. Our friends all commented on it—the women with envy, the men reproachfully.

He was creative, active, and a doer, thrived on challenges . . . then slowly, almost imperceptible, the change . . .

Double vision, black-outs (even when he was working on roofs in the flue business), numbness and swelling in the fingers, headaches . . . endless tests, all inconclusive . . . diagnosed with MS—no cure, just B12 shots—and a wife and six children dependent on him. Terrifying! Major life style changes—he now with an indoor job, which relied heavily on figures, math, and finances. I went to work (a blow to his ego, his manhood—he deeply resented it, blamed me). We hired someone part-time to supervise the children after school. Life was skewed, rushing off kilter, affecting everybody. Sol's problems escalated: visual perceptual problems, couldn't see things in a straight line—clumsy fingers couldn't handle buttons—numbers wouldn't come out right, checking account didn't balance—bill collectors at the door. Tense years passed with more testing . . . then . . . wrong diagnosis . . . definitely not MS . . . brain damage, blood couldn't get to it as it should . . . new regimen . . . arrested the progression but couldn't repair the damage or its effects. Couldn't compute any longer at work, had to leave the job on a disability retirement. Had a compulsion to control in the same measure he was losing control in his daily life. Assertive progressed to aggressive, then to hostile and belligerent. He denigrated sales people, clerks, waitresses, then the children. Argumentative, volatile, bullying-refused help—friends fell off—fearful, frightening, stifling, smotheringly dependent. Behavior swiftly spun out of control. He became a monster.

The sanctity of family was so ingrained in my world, it allowed no options to contemplate or even imagine. With this alien creature as an integral part of my life, I was terrified and I was changing, adjusting, accommodating, overlooking, and becoming inured and insensate. I was awash, frustrated, choking with resentment, with anger building to rage, while, at the same time, I was burning with feelings of intense and overwhelming guilt. I felt trapped, imprisoned, with no road map, no guide to my release. My lover was dead. I missed him, longed for him. I was not permitted to mourn for him because his body looked the same, moved the same, as though he still inhabited it. But it wasn't true. He did not. He was gone, but there was no closure.

Our marriage broke up, but not in time for the children, who are left with lasting emotional scars that have been and still are affecting their lives. His physical problems escalated—stroke—visual impairment—difficulty adjusting in an assisted living home—heart attack—death. After more than forty years of marriage, it was still hard for me to remember the good times—so overshadowed had they become with the lasting effects of the bad ones. Perhaps, if I had been permitted to mourn the passing of the person he was—to make a separation between that person and the one he became—maybe—some years could have been salvaged. How sad. A waste. A tragedy. Yet I could not shed a tear for him.

PART SIX

BONUSES

CHAPTER 42

THE GRANDS

"Toby doesn't need David to have a baby," asserted JoAnn. "A week or two after I announce I'm pregnant, so is she!" And it seemed like she was right. At least the timing would lead you to believe so. There were only fifteen days between her Keith, the first grandkid, and Toby's Tavis, the second grandkid. The same held true for the second go-around—twenty-three days between JoAnn's Brian and Toby's twins, Brandon and Cameron. And here I had promised to give a week a baby to help the new mamas. So I made the supreme sacrifice and rearranged my work schedule. Some sacrifice! It gave me a chance to be close to the babes, which was fun and interesting. And my, how different the cousins were and still are!

When I tried cuddling the first two grandkids, Keith reared back stiff as a board, and Tavis snuggled in for the duration. The contrast was amazing. The same held true for the other three grandkids—the Newman "boards" and the Jacome "snugglers." I would have felt miserably inadequate and unhappy because of the resistance of the "boards" had it not been for the "snuggling" three.

Their way of playing was also very different. The Newman boys spent endless time with their little toy cars, running them on the arms and backs of the chairs and spinning great tales about where the cars were going and for what purposes. They had car races and chases and crashes and awesome tricks. Their imaginations knew no bounds.

The Jacome boys did a kind of hug-wrestling, with a lot of laughs and giggles, and were into sports big-time, mostly as participants but also as observers. They drew people to them, many of whom became friends of a lifetime.

During the children's visits to my house when they were very young, they played together in the playpen, happily. When they were older and bigger, their playing field became the floor and the outdoors. They got along very well together. I thoroughly enjoyed being a spectator to their antics.

The Newmans, JoAnn's family, lived on the opposite side of town from me, and we rarely saw one another except at family gatherings. I've never gotten to know Keith very well. Although it was minimal, we had sporadic contacts when he was in high school. Like many teenagers (mine included), he was at times, exasperating. For example, after he finished high school, he went to Alaska to work for a time. When he returned, Karen, his girlfriend, had moved from Arizona to New York. While he collected enough money to follow her, he stayed at my house—until he broke my cardinal rule several times. He did not close the gate, which allowed my beautiful, loveable dog to get out when there was no one there to get her back in. After the fourth time and many warnings, I brought the dog in and put Keith out.

What I do know of him is that he is extremely bright, has been since he was very young. He enjoys music, plays the guitar and piano. He likes to learn and seems to be a perpetual student. History is his thing, and he is exceedingly good at it. I was able to witness this about eight or ten years ago when he and his family came to town to visit. I was living in a senior retirement community, and one of the activities was classes sponsored by the university. One day when Keith was visiting in town, the history facilitator was unable to attend to do his job. I asked Keith if he would be willing to fill in, and he was superb. After introducing himself to the class in a way that won him over from the start, he named the topic for this session and began his lecture. He did it clearly, seamlessly, with passion. He then encouraged and led a discussion. When the class was over, almost every one of the participants asked if it would be possible to have him take over the course on a permanent basis. He told me he would like to but had to return home.

Keith and Karen had moved to Connecticut, where Karen's family lives. They married there in 1999, and the ceremony and party were lovely. Karen is a social worker and Keith is a teacher. He has his master's and teaching degree. They have two delightful children, Lucy and Dexter, about whom you will hear later.

Brian, Keith's younger brother, is very thoughtful. He stayed overnight at my house once when he was in early grade school. In the morning I found him sitting quietly in front of the TV watching one of the pleas to help the starving children in Africa. His opening remark when he saw me was, "They shouldn't do that." When I asked why, he told me it would upset the balance of nature. Brian is exceedingly bright and he walks to his own drummer. He doesn't make friends easily, is a risk taker, and enjoys challenging people, mostly himself. He has a great sense of humor, though it's sometimes quirky enough that you're not sure how to take it. He had a bout with drugs when in high school and lived for a while with his Uncle Scott after his stint in a rehab program. I visited them briefly and had a chance to talk to Brian alone to ask how he liked living with his uncle. He said it was fine because, although Scott was tough, he was fair. Brian is a very hard worker, a loving father of three—two boys, Zander and Caden, and one girl, Ava. More about them later.

Next is Toby's family. Her oldest son Tavis is the handsome, strong, silent type. He was the responsible one who watched over his brothers and mother after his parents divorced when he was five and his brothers were two. He worked delivering newspapers and was heavy into sports. Football was his game and I didn't want to watch him practice because I didn't like the injuries kids sustained at that time. Once when I was visiting them when he was eleven or so, Toby took me to practice against my protestations. All was well for a while; then, Tavis was tackled to the ground, and two or three members of his team carried him off the field to the sidelines, where they seated him on a bench, took off his socks, and put ice packs around his ankles. After a bit they took the packs off, sprayed his feet and started putting his socks back on. I said to Toby in horror, "They are putting him back in the game!" She said she knew that, and I asked what she was going to do about it. She replied she would do nothing but, if I wanted to go in the field to stop it from happening, he would never talk to me for the rest of his life. I remained planted in my seat, because Toby knew her boys.

Her identical twin boys looked and sounded so alike that they played tricks on others. Once when I was visiting, I was having fun talking to one of the twins. He was sitting on their deep-seated, thick-cushioned couch. Suddenly, there was an eruption—like an earthquake— and a lot of giggling and laughing as the other twin pulled himself up and out of the seat of the couch. It turned out the one I was talking to was not the one who had been answering me, and I hadn't had a clue!

The twin I have known the best over the years is Brandon. He's the most outgoing loving and lovable boy/man to be with. Although we didn't live in the same city after the family's move to California, he visited frequently, bringing some of his friends with him. They especially enjoyed snowboarding in Colorado. An incident I thoroughly enjoyed and recall often is when I told Brandon that he and his friends were going to have to treat me to a lobster dinner—my absolutely favorite meal—because I had been feeding them for many days, and it was my turn now. He protested pitifully, stating how costly my meal would be and how they wouldn't be able to get anything for themselves to eat because, after paying for me, they couldn't afford it. I said not to worry—they could have bread and water for free. I was relentless.

As we waited for my lobster at the chosen restaurant, they reminded me that I was having the chef kill a living thing just because I wanted to eat only that, and I said I knew that and I was sorry. As I was eating the lobster, they began playing with the pieces of shell. Friend Marty was using parts to make a large nose and other appendages to his face, which was quite a sight. We were full of laughter. A family sitting a few tables away from us were watching our every move, trying to see what was so funny. Finally, the father of that family leaned over so far to see, he fell head to the ground. That did it! We were hysterical, and a good time was had by all.

Brandon works hard, plays hard, enjoys arranging parties, vacations, all kinds of get-togethers with his very many friends. He dated a lot but didn't keep the girls on the string, took his time deciding with whom he wanted to spend the rest of his life and made a good choice, Lita. He's the kind of guy who can fire you and you thank him.

Cameron has not been in my life except on rare family occasions. He liked school when he was young, was a good student but gradually lost interest. He liked sports, loves paddling, is friendly, and he found his niche in Hawaii, where he moved sixteen or eighteen years ago. When he comes back to the mainland, he comes to be with his family in California. I'm so pleased that I will be getting to see him more, since I moved to Sacramento. He is fantastic at construction. He, with the help of his brothers, made a marvelous ramp for me at the house we just moved from. And he did the same at the house we just moved *to*. I have a ramp that enables me to get into the sunken fireplace room in the house and another ramp just on the outside of the house. I ride it from the backyard to the driveway out front so I can get in the car.

He also helped his brothers make an awesome room, or rooms, out of the old ugly basement at Brandon's house when he was living there. They turned it into a game room with a bar, and added a bathroom with a shower and a laundry room. It's now a rental, since Brandon bought a house for himself and Lita. Cameron fittingly does construction for a living in Hawaii. The really fun thing he likes to do in Hawaii is paddle, and he actively participates in the races.

At this point, there were five grandsons, no girls. Then, to our surprise and delight came Taylor, my one and only granddaughter, courtesy of Diane. She was a beautiful baby, with brown hair and big brown eyes, and she continues to be a beautiful adult. She became the center of Diane's universe, and Diane did an outstanding job with her. I have three favorite stories about her when she was very young. Here they are:

1. Diane adorned Taylor, the only white child in her preschool, with a huge, lovely red ribbon in her hair on graduation day. The parents took many pictures, and she proudly showed hers off to one and all exclaiming, "Look! You can tell which one I am because I have a red ribbon in my hair."

2. My next favorite was one Diane told. Taylor was waiting to go to preschool and Diane was in the bathroom. Taylor called through the door.

"Mama, you don't have to take me, just tell me the way to go."

Di played along to see where it went, gave very simple directions. She heard Taylor running, and then heard a run-run-thump, run-run-thump. Then came the opening of the front door, and then a weak knock on the bathroom door followed by a teary voice saying, "Mama . . . I can't fly!"

Di opened the door to an unhappy Taylor with a Mary Poppins–like umbrella and a very, very sad face.

3. Another of my favorite Taylor stories took place when she lived with me for about six months. I drove her to and from her school, which was a distance from me, so we had time to chat. One day when I picked her up to go home, I said,

"Tay, listen. That was my mother's favorite song."

"You had a mama!? Where is she?"

"She died."

"Why?"

"Because she was old and sick."

"Are you going to die?"

"Yes, some day, but not for a long time."

Pause. Then Taylor again.

"Am I going to die?"

"Yes, some day, but not for a long, long time. All living things die—birds, cows, horses, dogs, cats, flowers."

Long silence. End of ride. The next day, as we drove home again, I said, "I'll be glad when you learn to drive so you can take me around and I won't have to do it."

"No!"

"What do you mean "no"? How come? I pick you up and take you to a lot of places. Why won't you do that for me?"

"You'll probably be dead by then."

That's a real show-stopper!

She had a wonderful opportunity when her dad, who'd been remodeling some apartments in France, invited her to come clean the apartments for him. The second night she was there, she met a handsome, charming young Frenchman. When her dad returned to the States, she remained in France with her boyfriend, knowing hardly anyone, without a job, without knowing the language. She's awesome! She learned the language, got jobs working in restaurants and bars, and was told by one of her bosses that he hired her because she spoke French so well.

She broke up with her boyfriend after a few years and now has another, from Lithuania. She is a young woman whose feet are solidly on the ground. She is undaunted by challenges. She's gregarious, engaging, appealing, outgoing, makes friends carefully, likes to travel, alone or with friends, to see new lands and experience different cultures. She has been to Mexico, France, Spain, Italy, Austria, Belgium, Luxembourg, the Netherlands, Germany, Thailand, Laos, Cambodia, Vietnam, Singapore, Morocco—she is confident and fearless.

She hasn't yet decided what she wants as her life's work. She is a natural comedian. She and her aunts share many a belly laugh when she brings her marvelous sense of humor to town. She would like to work as a standup comic, and she'd make a good one! She has worked briefly in a comedy theater. She described her experience to me. You are given a *very* short timeframe in which to perform and, as you look out at the sea of unfamiliar faces belonging to people you are supposed to make laugh, a momentary chill goes through you, but once you begin, it's a blast! She also worked as a model and a photographer's assistant. Those are other options among many she is considering. I don't know how much longer I'm going to be hanging around, but I'd love to see how her life plays out. It will be wonderful because she is.

****

And now for the *great*-grandkids!! It starts with Brian's Zander. I was in shock when he became a teenager and he's now fifteen, taller than me, with the voice and muscles of a man! What I remember about Zan is taking him, and sometimes his friends, to and from karate lessons. And how mindful he was about how to help me—such as giving me an arm or lift in and out of the car, or folding my walker and putting it in or taking it out of the car.

I remember a day when karate was over and I was about to put the walker away before taking him home. He was very young, but he stopped me with a voice that brooked no disagreement. He got out of the car, raised his hand, and shouted, "Stop! I will do it!" and without further adieu, he did. I also remember a time that I had taken him to karate and his dad picked him up. His dad was clueless about the walker, so Zan pushed him aside, told him what he had to do, and between them both, the walker was put away and Dad learned how to do it. When I lived in a senior center, the boys visited me often, and when I got my electric scooter or power chair, Zan had a great time zooming around the halls on it until he was told he had to stop—it was against the rules to ride around like that. It put the residents who were walking around in danger. Though he was saddened by what he was told, he followed the rules and continued to ride it, but at a slower speed.

He has been a soccer player for years. He enjoys the game very much, and his coach is impressed with him. He was bumped up to the red team, which is the third-highest level. His greatest interest in school, other than girls, is in science and math. He would like to be a chemical engineer. He is also counting the hours until he gets his driver's license, which will be very shortly, a matter of days. Zan continues to be a sweet, caring boy.

The little boy with the long hair and the big, big mind is Zan's kid brother Caden. He is my Renaissance great-grandson. He plays the piano, makes his own artistic things, writes, and wants to be a mechanical engineer. He thinks outside the box in a very adult manner for an eleven-year-old. And he is sweet and cuddly with his Nonny.

When he was a number of years younger, he was visiting his grandmother JoAnn, who was caring for a little girl. JoAnn had to go somewhere very close by for a very short time and left her in our care. I also had to go away for about fifteen minutes, so he was elected to watch over her. She was sobbing because the grandma had left. She knew Caden a little bit and me not at all. She was almost inconsolable. Caden patted her arm gently, spoke to her softly, assuring her his grandma would come back. He kept this up for almost a half hour until she became soothed enough to start playing with him. When I returned, a number of women who had witnessed it all went out of their way to let me know how impressed they were with him, and I was proud. He is a very lovable and caring boy.

Then, out of the blue, there's Ava, a beautiful little gal. She is the happiest baby I have ever seen, always with a smile or a laugh out loud. I haven't had the pleasure of meeting her in person yet, but I hear that she is walking around holding onto helping hands, at one year old. Maybe, if I'm lucky, she'll take a little stroll over here. In the meantime, she has her half-brothers Zan and Caden, Tyler and Kai to help her on her way.

Lucybelle, a.k.a. Lucy, Keith's daughter, was my second-born great-grandchild. The last time I saw her for a sizeable length of time was two years ago. Boys were her only interest. She followed her cousin Zander around constantly. We had no conversations about books, movies, TV programs, etc. She was a lovely-looking girl and still is from the pictures I've seen, but her likes and dislikes and interests are unknown to me.

The same is true of her younger brother Dexter. He is very bright, with interests beyond his age. We played Rumikub the last time we were together. It was his first time to play the game and he beat me quickly, fair and square. Unfortunately, I have not had the opportunity for a rematch or to get to know these children. Someday, perhaps.

Living in Sacramento, I've been able to see Tavis' beautiful, delightful three-year-old twins Skyler and Tate as they grow up. If you're looking for good entertainment, just settle back and watch and converse with them. I'm convinced that Skyler went to modeling school before she was born. She assumes the appropriate position the moment she hears a camera click. Tate is the comedian.

He twists his body and face into weird and laughable positions, and then he laughs along with you. They have been going to school . . . a pre-preschool program they both enjoy tremendously. They are learning their numbers and letters, and they are proud. And so are we of the two of them.

Now I have introduced you to my treasures, my children, grandchildren, great-grandchildren. Phew!!!!!! Now it's time for me to take a very long nap. I earned it. I deserve it. And I enjoyed every minute of it.

CHAPTER 43

THE DIVIDENDS

GRANDKIDS AND GREAT-GRANDKIDS

Mother Nature, that mischievous lass,

Deserves to go to the head of the class.

Although she didn't get it quite right

To my great pleasure and pure delight

She granted the wish I clearly did state

By setting the gender balance straight.

(Albeit a generation late).

With a huff and a puff in no more than a tick

And with twinkling eyes she did her shtick.

The first five grandkids, each a boy,

Fill me very full of joy.

Then, after a prolonged delay,

Another grandchild came my way,

A girl child, who lights up my day.

As though she hadn't done enough

With a flick of the wrist and a huff and a puff,

The next generation quickly appeared

Amidst throngs that whistled and loudly cheered.

With her leap in the air, and her mighty twirl

Came a great-grandboy and a great-grandgirl.

Then out of the oven, quick as could be,

Came a cuddly boy, great-grandbaby three.

Swiftly to join us, a cute boy did soar,

Making the count great-grandbaby four.

Then, goodness gracious, not one but two more:

Girl and boy twins for us to adore.

Thought that was the end, final curtain, fini,

Mother Nature said, "No, not so, you'll see,

Here comes beauty seven, and she's sweet as can be."

How many more? I haven't a clue.

When Mother Nature tells me, I'll share it with you.

So kudos to that Nature dame—

I'd put her in the Hall of Fame.

GRANDS

Back: Keith and Tavis
Front: Brian, Brandon and Cameron

Taylor

GREAT GRANDS

Caden, Zander, Ava,
Dexter and Lucy —
JoAnn's grandchildren.

Tate and Skyler —
Toby's grandchildren.

PART SEVEN

LAST WORDS: NOSTALGIA

CHAPTER 44

NOSTALGIA

In the days of penny postcards and three-cent stamps, we were pretty spoiled. Everything was delivered free to the house. Coal came weekly and was noisily sent down the chute to the basement in a cloud of dust so it could be shoveled daily into the furnace. The iceman, with a protective cloth over his shoulder, brought a large chunk of ice in his tongs to be put into the top of the icebox before we had refrigerators. We used to snatch ice chips off the trucks in the heat of summer. Milk was delivered in glass bottles, with the milk on the bottom and cream on the top, before the days of homogenization. It was placed in the milkbox at the side of the house with one little door to the outside for the milkman and one inside for the customer. Even in that protected environment it would freeze in the chill of winter, expanding and pushing the cap off the top. (Much later, in Arizona, the milkman placed the milk directly into the refrigerator so it wouldn't sour in the intense heat.)

We played with kids in the neighborhood after school and on the weekends. The girls' games were jacks and jump-rope, while the boys' was touch football. Hopscotch; 1, 2, 3 Baseball; and Kick the Can were gender neutral, so girls and boys pursued them together. We lined up at the curbs shouting, "Red Rover, Red Rover let so-and-so come over" and tried to tag the person crossing the street. Kissing games like Spin the Bottle and Truth or Consequences were daring and filled with titters and giggles.

We rode bikes, one speed because there were no others, roller-skated on the clunky old skates that attached to our shoes when we clamped them tight with our keys, and our ice skates also attached to our shoes but not sturdily. During Halloween, we had more days than just tricks or treats. There was doorbell night, when we'd stick a pin in the bell so it would ring nonstop. The nasty one was garbage night, when we'd collect it, put it in a paper bag, wet it, and toss it on a neighbor's roof, someone who had given us a hard time. Of course, that brought on an even harder time for us.

The highlight of each week was the Saturday matinee at the neighborhood movie house. Talk about bang for the buck! For a thin little dime, we got a newsreel, short-shorts like Robert Benchley's demonstration of sleep, serials of the cliffhanger variety, like *Fu Manchu*, and double features, which were two full-length movies. The earliest feature I remember was a silent movie, the only one I ever saw, called *Seventh Heaven* and starring Janet Gaynor and Charles Farrell. It was a sad love story during World War I in which the hero was blinded in the war. It was heart wrenching and romantic. And I can still taste the ice cream cones with jimmies on top of the two scoops of ice cream securing the surprise ball of hard candy at the bottom of the waffle cone.

If we went to a movie that was not within walking distance, we took the streetcar for ten cents (there were no buses then). We could get transfers for free, which enabled us to switch from one streetcar to another so we could almost travel the whole city for that same little dime. Buffalo's winter snow and ice challenged the streetcars, often causing them to go off the track. We got out, lifted them back on the tracks and resumed our ride.

But the same snow was fun in other ways, because the schools closed. That left us free to kick the crust off the top of the snow to uncover the hydrants for the fire department and to push cars out of drifts. Then there were the dangerous, foolhardy things we did that our parents knew nothing about, like hitching our sleds to the backs of trucks so we could be towed along on the slick ice until the driver discovered us. Never occurred to us we could be pulled under the wheels and killed. Or, when we learned to drive, slamming on the brakes on an icy patch in an isolated area so we could spin the car around.

And speaking of cars, although our stick-shift cars before automatic transmissions weren't very big, their capacity was enhanced by the running boards, which accommodated as many as could fit and hang on tight. For romance, there were the rumble seats. They were designed to be two-seaters but more could squeeze in in a pinch, and it did pinch. We all pitched in to help the driver pay for the gas, which cost ten cents a gallon.

Travel out of town was by car or train, rarely by bus, and planes for regular people weren't even on our horizon yet. When they were, my first flight was with a friend in college who had just gotten his pilot's license. He took me up in an open-cockpit plane, skimmed over the tops of the trees, zoomed up and down and upside-down to try to scare me half to death. It didn't work. I loved it. My only objection was to the extreme noise.

Travel to Canada was mostly by car over the Peace Bridge, Rainbow Bridge, or Niagara Falls Bridge.

Sometimes we took the ferry or the Crystal Beach boat, which was lovely. It was a double-decker with a jukebox and place to eat and we could walk around, socialize, stand at the railing and enjoy looking at Lake Erie before it was polluted. It was cleaned up the last time I saw it.

I thought Canada was a suburb of Buffalo until I almost reached adulthood. Even then, I wasn't really convinced it was a separate country until my trip to Montreal, where French was the order of the day. We spent most

Irma and friends at Bay Beach, Canada, 1937.

summers on the beaches of Canada. I played on the amusements as a child, especially the rollercoaster at the

Grove at Crystal Beach, and so did my children, but not as often because we couldn't afford the money or the time by then. My mouth still waters at the thought of the large, flat cinnamon suckers I enjoyed there.

The Grove is gone now, replaced by a large golf course or tennis court. We would sun on the rocks at Bay Beach and swim in the lake there. Had to walk what seemed like miles to get to deep enough water to swim because of the many sandbars. For an invigorating swim we drove or hitchhiked to the Quarry. There was no bottom that any of us ever found, and the water was icy cold and clear. We danced in the large ballroom at Crystal Beach, but my favorite was the smaller Royal ballroom at Bay Beach. The times were carefree, made for hayrides, bonfires, and roasting marshmallows. That's how my friend, Sasha, and I

Sasha's and Irma's 16th birthday party – 10/37

celebrated our sixteenth birthdays. We were born on the same day, same year. She had a better time than I because her mother said, "Have a nice time, dear," and my mother said, "Make sure your friends have a nice time at your party, dear."

A dance attraction in Buffalo, or perhaps it was the suburb Ellicott Creek, was a milk bar, which was a wonderful place for teens. It was set up like a nightclub bar, with booths lining the walls and surrounding a large dance

Bob and friends after a swim in the creek.

floor. Soft drinks, milkshakes, and sodas were the beverages, nothing alcoholic. A jukebox or, on occasion, a live band supplied the music. The most memorable evening was the night a handsome pianist was playing soulful music to himself. It was Eddie Duchin, not long after the death of his wife. It was sad and incredibly sentimental.

Later on there was the farm, my mother's idea, supported by Dad and Bob. It was in the Boston Hills

about an hour out of Buffalo, near Springville, and it was a beautiful setting. Rolling green hills, a running creek deep enough for swimming but not diving, a house and land and, in the beginning, livestock. We were so totally ignorant about farming and country life in general that we provided our

Dad in front of the vegetable garden.

neighbors with endless hours of entertainment, though they were polite enough not to laugh at us in our

presence. When the rooster died, we thought the hens would no longer be able to lay eggs. When my brother wanted to mate

Horsing around in front of the farmhouse.

our swayback old mare, he walked her a mile up the hill to a farm with a stud. He walked her slowly back down again without success because she "wasn't ready"—she wasn't in heat.

My family loved the whole thing; I hated it. You don't take a teenage girl out of the big city and plunk her on an isolated farm. The most hellish day was when the family left me with a non-housebroken puppy and asked me to take care of him and to pasteurize the milk and clean the house. As soon as they were out of sight, the heavens opened up and the rain came down and the heifer got out of the pasture and the puppy got out of his enclosure. I cleaned up after the dog, enclosed him again, and went out to deal with the cow. I sloshed over to her through the mud, talked to her, reasoned with her, begged her to get out of the vegetable garden and stop eating the produce, but she ignored me. I slipped and slid into the barn, got a rope, and tied it around her neck and pulled. For each step forward, she pulled me two or three steps back.

When I was thoroughly drenched and ankle deep in mud, she decided on her own to return to pasture. I heaved a sigh of relief, returned to the house, the shower, the cleaning, the pasteurizing, and the sun came out and the rain went away and a friend from the city drove up. We went to Springville for sodas, had a lovely visit; he drove me back home and left. The sun went down, the rains came back, the cow got out of pasture, and we had a re-run of the previous struggle. When the heifer was back in the pasture and I was rain soaked and muddy, my family returned. I will refrain from repeating the expletives I used in my greeting to them.

It wasn't all bad. I did enjoy swimming in the creek and pulling ears of corn off the stalks and cooking and eating them. There was one particularly amusing time after I was married when a couple of friends joined us in a visit to the farm. It was Saturday night, and we walked down the road a piece to the barn where the weekly dance was in progress. Our intent was to go as spectators. As we were settling into our seats, our friend Bob was attacked by a five-by-five, powerful katrinka who asked, "Square, mister?" Before he could process her words to form a reply, he was lifted from his feet, doe-see-doed and swung all around the floor, and never touched down until she deposited him, red-faced and in shock in front of us. We got out of harm's way as quickly as we could navigate Bob through the door.

The media was different in those days, slower. The entertainment center of yesteryear was the lovely wood console radio-record player, no TV yet. We listened to news, soaps like *Ma Perkins* and *My Gal Sal* and mysteries like *Inner Sanctum*, *The Lone Ranger*, *Mr. District Attorney* and *Mr. Keene, Tracer of Lost Persons*, as well as comedians like Jack Benny, Fanny Brice as Baby Snooks, and Fred Allen—all on the radio.

We heard and danced to the rhythm and music from both the radio's *Hit Parade* and our record collection. The big, heavy 78 records and the smaller and lighter 45s played anything from Caruso's "Pagliacci" and Lawrence Tibbet's "Volga Boatman" to popular songs like "The Music Goes Down and Around," "Red Sails in the Sunset," and "I'll Never Smile Again."

We were moved by King Edward's abdication speech when he gave up his throne to be with the woman he loved which, though the reception was rough and scratchy, was remarkably romantic. And it was over the

radio in the smoking room in the basement of my
dormitory in Cleveland where we were shocked by news,
delivered in sonorous tones by FDR, of the infamous
bombing of Pearl Harbor. We didn't see the devastation
until we could view it at the movies on a newsreel.

Dad had one of the early and very difficult wire
recorders on which he used to dictate. He went from that
to a transcriber with small green plastic disks. He read a
letter onto one of the disks written by Bob shortly before
Israel's War for Independence. Bob was in Palestine
during the British Mandate when he joined a group of
Jews going to the Wailing Wall (Western Wall) in
Jerusalem on the High Holidays. He described with
passion how the British ill-treated and, in some cases, beat
the Jews as they tried to blow the Shofar near the Western
Wall. We transferred the letter onto a tape, which I still
have. I'm not sure about the transcriber but I do know
that son Scott has the wire recorder.

When TV finally entered our home on a 10-inch
screen in black and white, it amazed us. We were glued to
Texaco's Uncle Milty (Milton Berle) and the *Show of Shows*
with Sid Ceaser and Imogene Coca, and Ed Sullivan's

variety show, *Playhouse 90*, and Howdy Doody and Mickey Mouse. Even so, we wouldn't have believed that it would become so all-consuming, that the "breaking news" happens right in your living room.

These are a few of the memories that spun right off. I could spin more, but I trust these have conveyed the flavor, which was my intent.

CHAPTER 45

THE LATEST MOVES

I've never been known for boundless energy, even in the cold, but heat enervated me. It laid me low, wiped me out, I couldn't take it. Yet it took me forty-one years to get out of the Arizona oven. I made my first visit to Denver in the 1960s to attend a conference to hear Drs. Kemp and Helfer talk about their breakthrough book regarding battered child syndrome. The conference, concepts, and environs were impressive.

Subsequently, years later, I visited Debbie and then JoAnn, who had both put roots into this community. I was taken by the green, the trees, other vegetation—and the cool. Instead of using the wisdom that is supposed to accompany old age, I chose to buy a house rather than move into a condo or similar place where someone else is responsible for maintenance, not me. I thought it was a reasonable decision because I wanted a dog, a big one, and they are not allowed in most such living quarters. And so, in September of 1997, Toby helped me sort, discard, and pack the belongings from my house of forty-one years so the buyers could move in. Susan and Bill

chauffeured me in my not-so-trusty Toyota from Tucson
to Denver. As Bill succinctly put it, "It was a trip from
hell!" The temperature hit 100 degrees, as did our internal
thermostats. The radiator cracked, leaked, steamed—no
more AC—and we had to stop for infusions of water in
the many tiny towns along the way until we replaced the
radiator in Albuquerque. We did get to our destination,
nonetheless, and had many laughs along the way. JoAnn
helped me settle my belongings into my "new-to-me"
house. A month later, JoAnn's number-two son Brian

Mindy (back) and friend, Quimby.

accompanied me to the Dumb Friend's League (terrible
name), where I adopted Mindy, my sweet German
Shepherd/Aussie mix, constant companion.

It took no longer than the first year to re-learn
what I had completely blocked out of my memory bank

from my life in Buffalo. Grass must be fertilized, watered and mowed. Trees (nine of them in my back yard alone) must be pruned, and leaves must be raked and disposed of. Crab apple and apricot trees were outside my realm of experience. Their blossoms are beautiful in the spring, but the fruit is a terrible bother. The lovely, clean white stuff that falls from the sky at expected and totally unexpected times requires shoveling, and its accompanying ice needs chopping. These are not the activities that old, arthritic bodies thrive on!

Nobody revealed to me Denver's versatility. I had no idea, when change of seasons was mentioned, they often happen in one twenty-four hour period. To my surprise, I discovered my body could no longer expand and contract from heat to cold as quickly as it did years ago. My doctor tried to fill my request for a lube job but couldn't find a place to perform it on people. They are really missing a bet! His alternate suggestion was water exercises, so I obediently joined a club with a pool and classes for arthritis sufferers. If you use an alphabetic scale, exercise has always been my "Z" priority.

Fortunately, there were some very nice co-sufferers in the class who became my friends.

Once I was settled, it was time to add new friends. Aside from the children, who have busy lives, I knew no one here. I contacted the Jewish Community Center to see about bridge clubs. None were at an hour that appealed to me. I was then told of a program for Seniors called VIVA!, which is sponsored by the Denver University. It was a marvelous discovery. Their classes on a multitude of subjects were held during the day, and a major part of their appeal for me, who'd never liked school, was no exams, no term papers, no grades. What could be more ideal?! So I signed up and took classes thereafter. Some of the classes I took were the Supreme Court; the Bill of Rights; Mystery Stories; Jazz; Swing; Short Stories; and, my favorite of all, Writing—memoir, creative, and poetry. My colleagues were a wonderful, stimulating group of people from a variety of backgrounds, everyone contributing in a most delightful way.

The philosophy in the old children's song, "Make new friends and keep the old" is a good one, but most problematic the older you get. It's the "keeping" part that is difficult due to the ever-increasing incidence of sickness and death. Would that you *could* keep the old! My social calendar was not overwhelming, but it kept pace with the slow-down of the housing that encases me. It should not be construed that time lay heavy on my hands. It flew. I could never harness it sufficiently to complete the many things on my "to-do" list. So my life revolved around classes, water exercises, reading, writing, an occasional movie or play, lunch or dinner with friends, and the usual menial type of shopping—grocery, primarily. And I looked out on the pretty green grass and the stately trees or the snow-covered winter scene in my private park otherwise known as my backyard and I watched the cavorting of the squirrels and the birds and life was good.

Then came the falling, not of leaves but of me. After about three or four falls, I thought it would be best to give up my house and move into a senior living center, so I did. It was easy to make friends, to give up cooking and cleaning, and take part in activities I enjoyed. After a year or so, JoAnn moved to a different apartment next door to a different senior facility She checked it out, took the tour, got the brochures, and gave them to me as she told me she thought I'd like it better. It was much more relaxed and had many more activities to offer and was cheaper. I went to see it, walked in, felt at home, and moved in. It was great! Within the first year, I joined the book club, participated in the discussion group, played Rumikub, enjoyed happy hour and the live entertainment they had, and became president of the resident council. And in March of 2012, I moved out.

I haven't mentioned "The Committee." It is activated when my children are concerned about me. They arrange conference calls on the phone from Tucson, Santa Fe, Denver, and Sacramento to discuss "what to do about Mom." The most recent concern was after my ninetieth birthday, when I had bronchitis. I was living in a wonderful world, enjoying it very much, but the cost of the care I was going to need was more than I could afford. After in-depth discussions, which took place outside of my presence, they decided I should move to Sacramento and live with Toby, who would become my caregiver. When they shared their plan with me—which they had to do because I have veto powers—it didn't take me long to agree, and I couldn't have found a better caregiver if I'd searched the planet. I have joined a senior writing group—mostly memoirs—and will look for other activities and friends when I get my land legs. I am having a marvelous time being with my daughter, two of her sons, their wives, and the adorable girl and boy great-grandkids. What a wonderful life!

CHAPTER 46

I BEQUEATH (To My Children)

The longer I live, the less I can leave

Of trinkets and silver and gold,

Of the hands-on, material, earthly things,

Whether new or from days of old.

I think you'll remember my passing,

Whether I bequeath you something or not.

But it still would be nice, like sugar and spice,

To leave something—but what have I got?

The memories we had, some good and some bad,

Are different for each lass and lad.

But these you inherit, automatically merit,

Like a gift that you already had.

But there is a gift I was left by my dad

That stood him in very good stead.

And I must say it's been very handy for me

As it's helped me to move right ahead.

It's not a thing you can touch, smell, or feel

But it's strong, lasted two generations,

Probably more, if someone kept score,

It was kind of like dad's pre-oration.

It was dad's high school motto; he recited it oft

To the point that it made us quite weary.

But to get a job done, though it's not always fun,

This adage works surely and clearly:

Pay heed to me, kids, lend your ears one and all;

When I'm at the end, when I make my last call,

This motto's true blue, I can state with assurance,

So practice it, learn from it, it's your insurance:

Perseverance DOES conquer all!

CHAPTER 47

THE WRAP-UP

It is difficult to shrink a little more than nine decades of personal stories into a little book that someone might be interested to thumb through. Especially when the central figure of the piece is not a celebrity or renowned for an outstanding discovery or invention, but is only a regular person who is unique, as all people are unique. So what is my great sense of urgency to get this out, and to whom? Let's parse this sentence. Was it requested? Yes, in a way, when I was working on our genealogy. A few of the children commented that it would be nice to know, but not to the extent they offered to pitch in and help. It is a humongous job, which I was unable to complete because of the brick wall I hit searching back beyond my grandparents. So what's my excuse? Do I need one? It's my need to tell, and the fun I have, for the most part, in the telling. The painful parts are not fun, but they need to be told.

The "to whom?" part of the question is my offspring, relatives, friends—and anyone on the street who might be interested, though I can't imagine why.

Who knows—there may be a few others like me interested in life-sharing information from one human being to another. Is there anything, after all, more interesting than people? I think not.

That leaves us with, "What is the urgency?" I have no idea how many miles I will be able to hike up the mountain, or when or if I will reach the top. After all, it isn't my plan to give it a straight shot to the summit. There are still some side paths I'd like to explore along the way. Also, there are more projects I want to finish before the final stop. As a matter of fact, I can even think of some I might like to start and then finish.

I was never a girl scout, and I was certainly not a boy scout (but close to it, because brother Bob shared his experiences so well). Nonetheless, my M.O. is to always be prepared. It would be a shame to miss an interesting, exciting adventure simply because you lolled around in bed too long or put off doing the laundry or feeding the dog or getting the groceries or any manner of other essential obligations that must be filled before you can take a step into the outside world. This won't happen to me because I am at the ready. I am going to publish this partial memoir just to know it has been completed. "Partial" is because I have barely scratched the surface, so be prepared for a sequel. Don't get too anxious, though, because my poetry is next on the agenda, to be followed by some fictionalized cases from my years of gainful employment.

I learned long ago that you can't pour anything out of an empty bucket. That's why I need reading time and classes to stimulate the gray cells so I can replenish the contents of the bucket. This broken-down casement of a body that houses me moves ever so slowly to the point it almost seems as though I am moving backward. That's when I try this walking bit. I am terrific at sitting, especially in front of my computer, and my arthritic fingers move very quickly over the keys trying to keep up with my fairly agile mind. Isn't that a kick!

The vignettes I have written for this book are not all of special significance. Some are, and others just tickled my fancy or came to the fore for an unexplainable reason. As Jimmy Durante used to say, "I've got a million of them!" Anyone who looks back over a ninety-year span has to have at least a million memories, unless they died somewhere along the way. And the memories are a mixed bag—the good, bad, funny and hateful—the mix of life and life, as I view it, is always interesting. So here's to it— L'Chaim.

CHAPTER 48

LAST WORDS

You can scatter me high or dig me deep

Or toss me in a garbage heap.

Whatever you do, make sure it's cheap,

If you don't and I know, it'll make me weep.

And here is a secret that you can keep:

It won't matter to me when I'm in the big sleep.

But once it's all over and what's said is said,

Just make damned sure that I really am dead!

About the Author

Irma Fisher was born in Buffalo NY in 1921, spent 41 years in the intense heat of the Arizona desert, then migrated to Denver and on to Sacramento, where she lives with her daughter/care giver, Toby. Her career choices at age 13 were marriage and a large family or social work. She had both: six children, six grandchildren, seven great grandchildren (as of this printing) and 20 years as a social worker. Now in her ninth decade, Irma delights in her third career as an author. Life, she notes, offers stimulating and fulfilling choices if you wish to partake of them; for as long as she's here, she intends to do just that.

* 9 7 8 1 6 2 1 3 7 6 5 0 7 *